NEWSPAPERS AND NEW MEDIA

by David A. Patten

D0814416

Knowledge Industry Publications, Inc.
White Plains, NY and London

Communications Library

Newspapers and New Media

Library of Congress Cataloging-in-Publication Data
Main entry under title:

Newspapers and New Media

    (Communications library)
    Patten, David A.
      Newspapers and new media.

    Bibliography: p.
    Includes index.
    1. Newspapers.   I. Title.
PN4731.P35   1985   070   84-26139
ISBN 0-86729-137-0
ISBN 0-86729-143-5 (pbk)

Printed in the United States of America.

10   9   8   7   6   5   4   3   2   1

Table of Contents

Figures

1

Overview

In 1981, at the annual convention of the American Newspaper Publishers Association (ANPA), cable television entrepreneur Ted Turner told his audience that his medium was more effective than theirs. Cutting down trees to publish newspapers, he argued, was an inherently inefficient business. His address left no doubt that he believed the days of newspapers were numbered.

Although Turner's opinions represented a somewhat radical viewpoint, it *was* already clear that the 1980s would bring extraordinary shifts to communications industries.

Many of these shifts are rooted in the proliferation of developing new media that were portending basic changes in the way established media—particularly newspapers—do business. Eventually these changes will not only influence technical processes, but will strike at editorial policies, news content, reporting methods, journalistic law and ethics—in short, every aspect of the journalism business.

For newspapers, these changes have long been foreshadowed by one overpowering statistic: declining household penetration. According to the U.S. Bureau of the Census, households in the United States increased by 148% between 1930 and 1977, from about 30 million to about 74 million. But newspaper circulation improved just 57% during that time, from 75,166,000 to 139,320,000. To put the statistics another way, the circulation per household dropped from about 1.32 in 1930 to about .84 in 1977. In dollars and cents this one-third drop in household penetration has resulted in billions of dollars of lost revenues for the newspaper industry.

John Morton, a former newspaper reporter and now a newspaper analyst with Lynch Jones & Ryan (a member of the New York Stock Exchange), attributes many of newspapers' competitive problems to matters of editorial quality and circulation:

1

> This entire scenario of rising competition and its aftereffects on newspapers developed because of poor circulation performance. In effect, poor household coverage became the "soft underbelly" of the newspaper industry. Shopper [free, non-subscription newspapers] owners and suburban publishers recognized this. The U.S. Postal Service, eager to increase its business, certainly recognized it.[1]

One outcome of the circulation declines of the early 1980s was that only so many newspapers could sustain profitability, especially when coupled with rising costs in fuel and in all production spheres. One by one, a number of newspapers that could not survive these two factors within the depressed economy found themselves going out of business, or cutting back severely on staff. Among the dailies that went under in 1982 were the *Cleveland Press,* the *Chicago Daily News,* the *Washington Star* and the *Philadelphia Bulletin.* Even some of the survivors suffered drastic casualties or underwent mutations: the *Des Moines Tribune* ceased its afternoon run and was partly absorbed by the *Register,* in the course of which the *Tribune* had to lay off an estimated 150 to 200 employees, 30 to 60 of these from the editorial staff; the demise of the afternoon *Minneapolis Star* led to the debut of the all-day *Minneapolis Star and Tribune;* the *Tonight* edition of the *New York Daily News* was canceled, and at one point the newspaper itself was briefly on the trading block; and in December 1982 Rupert Murdoch saved the *Boston Herald-American* from extinction, purchasing it minutes before it was due to close shop.[2] All in all, 28 newspapers ceased publication in 1982 alone. In 1983, 16 dailies stopped publishing; of these, 7 were suspended, 3 converted to weekly publication, and 6 merged with a sister paper. Two dailies were started in 1983, for a net loss for the year of 14, according to ANPA statistics.[3] Newspaper analyst J. Kendrick Noble, Jr., has projected that 74 more newspapers will drop out of the ballgame between now and the end of the decade.

The fear of decline and excitement over burgeoning new communications technologies resulted in a commitment to learning new methods. Editors and managers struggled with a new vocabulary that included such terms as cable TV, videotex, database publishing, LPTV (low-power television) and direct broadcast from satellite. Some called the lingo "videospeak," and many journalists longed for the days when the alphabet was used to form words rather than acronyms. But whether or not they liked or even accepted the implications for their trade that went along with the technological innovations of the new media, they had no choice but to realize that times and tactics were changing.

In order to understand fully the climate in which new forms of communication wrought changes on newspapers (and other traditional media) we must first consider a few basic issues to clarify the present situation. These are:

(1) the factors shaping traditional communications media, especially news-papers, before the new technologies came on the scene; (2) the impact of the new media on the collective and individual journalistic self-image or sense of identity and (3) the long-term effects of the arrival of these new forms of communication (i.e., would they replace traditional media, change the old in some way or simply coexist with them).

INITIAL PHASE OF NEW MEDIA DEVELOPMENT

When we examine the initial phase of new media development, a period that can be said to extend roughly from the rise of satellite-distributed cable programming networks in 1975 to the cable-newspaper boom of 1982—we are struck most by the sense of uncertainty about traditional media. Cable could be seen to be eroding a small but significant percentage of network television shares. The percentage of homes subscribing to newspapers continued to edge downward. Combined with an ailing economy, these trends gave rise to questions about the basic viability of that most profitable of advertising media, the newspaper. This fear of decline, and reaction against it have had a lasting influence on new media development.

News magazine cover stories about the abundance of cable television, along with reports of personal computers, robots, the space shuttle and other high-tech advances, made the new media appear to be part of a snowball effect.

It is difficult to recall that only two decades ago, technology was viewed with great suspicion by the nation's young people. They feared it might fatally disrupt the ecological balance of the planet, or might be used to invade privacy and control dissent. Some of this concern is reflected in an early, classic book on cable television, *The Wired Nation*. In 1972 Ralph Lee Smith wrote about the potential evils of cable TV: "Everyone's comings and goings can be monitored every minute and hour of the day. Will this new form of police power be properly used? Should it be limited, and if so, what should its limits be?"[4]

Smith's solution was a cable environment highly controlled by government. Cable should be built through massive government subsidies, similar to the interstate highway system, and should be regulated as a monopoly common carrier. "Unless the issues in these future uses of the cable are understood and faced, 1984 could easily come well in advance of George Orwell's prediction," Smith wrote.[5]

Yet as the 1980s arrived, the Federal Communications Commission (FCC) experienced a deregulatory spirit like none before. Futurists looked to tech-nology for solutions to world problems, and the political leadership empha-sized the private sector role in finding those solutions.

In his landmark book *The Third Wave,* Alvin Toffler wrote about forces that were bringing tremendous changes in social structure and communications. The first wave of these spread agriculture around the world and created permanent farming settlements. The second wave brought industry and complex economies, concentrating huge numbers of persons in the cities. The third wave, which according to Toffler, we are now in the midst of, is one of revolutionary technology, with a "smart environment" that literally converses with each of us on individual terms. Seen to be primary among the institutions that will be changed by this environment are the media.[6]

Toffler believes that increasing numbers of information sources, coupled with interactive systems that transform the viewer from a passive to an active media user, would result in a "demassification" of communications. This would change our very view of ourselves:

> The de-massification of the mass media—the rise of mini-magazines, newsletters, and small scale, often Xeroxed communications along with the coming of cable, cassette, and computer—shatters the standardized image of the world propagated by the Second Wave communications technologies and pumps a diversity of images, ideas, symbols and values into society.[7]

Toffler goes on to say that the demassified media were beating back the established media on many fronts. Those such as Ted Turner who questioned the viability of established journalistic institutions used Toffler's ideas to bludgeon their opponents.

EFFECT ON JOURNALISTS' SELF-IMAGE

Indeed, there were even some newspaper people who at the time expressed alarm at changing conditions, as reflected by the demise of so many newspapers. Mel Tinney, cable manager for the Eau Claire Press Co. in 1982, cautioned, "You do not have to lose that whole column of red called revenue to be in trouble. All you have to do is lose that little black part at the top called profit."[8] A staff writer for the *Tampa Tribune,* Steve Piacente, gained brief notoriety for commenting: "As a mullet-wrapper of the future, the newspaper is doomed."[9]

At the same time it was becoming evident that the communications industry could not expand fast enough to employ all the young people drawn to its ranks. With more than 70,000 students enrolled in journalism schools across the country, the economy of the early 1980s did not bode well for the next generation of journalists.

A growing pessimism resulted from the poor economy, the rise of the high-tech businesses and the failure of many established journalistic institutions. Some of this pessimism crept into the very foundation of the business—the working journalist.

In May 1982 the American Society of Newspaper Editors released preliminary findings examining the attitudes of newspaper journalists. Some 489 journalists answered a 17-page questionnaire, and 187 submitted to extensive interviews. The report suggested that journalists underestimated the importance of their own news coverage. For example, the journalists believed that about half of all adults read a newspaper each day. The actual average is more than two-thirds. Similarly, the journalists underestimated by about a third the amount of time the average reader spends reading a weekday newspaper.

Also, most newspeople (54%) wrongly perceived that watching television news tends to decrease newspaper readership. Forty percent agreed with the statement: "I feel readers in the future will more and more turn to other media that better meet their needs."

The researchers concluded that "At worst, the overestimation of the public's dependence on broadcast and the underestimation of the importance of print may bring about what print people fear most: Public dependency on electronic journalism."[10]

Exactly how this negative self-image occurred in an industry that, with the fall of Richard Nixon, had gained political and economic clout is hard to determine. Television's coverage of visually impressive, momentous news events may be one cause. Newspaper reporters may have felt they could not keep pace with it.

Suddenly journalists, who had made change one of their bread-and-butter themes over the years, risked being branded as ill equipped for change themselves. Ironically, during this period journalistic coverage of science and technology reached an unprecedented level. But the coverage could not erase the impression of decline caused by flat audience and circulation figures, rising costs, gradually decreasing market share of advertising and the occasional splash of a newspaper's failure. Moreover, there seemed to be a general feeling that the future of the world depended more on electronics, computers and satellites than on the reliable old newspapers delivering word of these.

Displacement or Coexistence?

In retrospect, it is interesting to note that Toffler did not predict the demise of the established media. He believed the path to future communications would be wide, accommodating both the old and the new media. If established media ceased to exist, the old mass media would be replaced by the new mass media, thwarting demassification.

Yet, even by 1980, newspaper staff and management had been well acquainted with the more threatening notion that weaker media are destined to die out. This theory finds its basis in two facts and one inference. The first fact is that the percentage of the nation's gross national product spent on public relations, advertising and promotion has remained a remarkably consistent 2.0 to 2.5% for several decades. The second is that the number of media taking a slice out of the economic pie is rapidly increasing. And the inference is that some established media are bound to perish if we are to make room for the new.

This overall concept, however, has two major flaws. First, it tends to dismiss the normative aspects of change—are we talking about change for its own sake, or change to improve the lot of people? Moreover, it assumes a static media environment.

Second, the theory tends to lack historical proof or precedent. The history of communications is hardly littered with examples of one medium utterly superseding another. Usually, an accommodation is reached between the old and the new, with each medium concentrating on what it does best relative to the other media in the overall communications environment.

The advent of radio and magazines did not wipe out books and newspapers; television did not wipe out radio; billboards, shoppers, direct mail and other forms have all sliced a secure piece of the revenue pie for themselves. While specialization has occurred—the afternoon form of the newspaper appears less viable due to transportation and fuel costs, and television—few media have actually been put on the endangered list.

The point is that our established media will survive the new media, though adaptation may be required. According to Doyle Dane Bernbach, the new media will coexist alongside the established media. Newspapers, for example, are expected to be widely involved in cable and electronic text services, and some will distribute national editions via satellite (as does *USA Today*). Also, newspapers are expected to target with greater frequency special areas of their circulation zones.

The theory of displacement—i.e., weaker media will die out—is not supported by fact but it *has* gained currency. The long-term effect of such a negative view remains to be seen. The biggest danger is that print journalists will react against it, becoming less open to change at the very time they must adapt most. Such a reactionary attitude *could* threaten newspapers. Veteran newspaperman David Shaw writes:

> The imminent demise of the daily newspaper has been predicted before, though, and as University of Texas journalism professor William

Mindak says, "History has proved most of these gloomy prognosticators wrong *IF* (and this is a big if) the media reacted intelligently and quickly to their changing environment."[11]

Newspapers *are* responding to their changing environment; whether their response will prove to have been quick enough—and intelligent enough—is something that can only be judged by future generations of readers . . . and nonreaders.

There are growing signs that newspapers will not be defeated by pessimism. The first of these is newspaper involvement in the new media, which demonstrates a willingness to explore new communications systems. Second, there is a growing trend toward newspaper entrepreneurialism, both in print and nonprint information. Finally, we now see new training efforts in journalism schools across North America. At the University of Florida, San Diego State, Brigham Young, Western Ontario and others, students are learning to use the new tools of their trade, including the character generator and the videotex computer terminal. These trends show that newspapers will remain healthy, growing institutions for years to come. Or as Katharine Graham, Chairman of the Washington Post company, has declared, "We are not quite ready for the obit page just yet."[12]

The doom-and-gloom atmosphere surrounding newspaper publishing in the early 1980s did force a basic reevaluation of the newspaper's worth. Examining newspapers from top to bottom, newspaper professionals rediscovered their value as inexpensive, detailed public records that fulfill a much-needed watchdog role. Said Sydney Gruson, vice chairman of *The New York Times*:

> When you hear the next prophecy about the fall of the newspaper business, ask yourself: What carries 30 million bits of storable information, weighs less than three pounds, provides hard copy, handles both text and graphics, allows random access, is available 24 hours a day, is completely portable and costs less than 30 cents a connect-hour (because it is paid for mostly by someone other than the customer)? It is not the latest piece of fancy computer hardware. It is . . . the daily newspaper.[13]

NEWSPAPERS ADAPT TO COPE WITH THE NEW MEDIA

For decades the entertainment-information business has been dominated by newspapers, television and radio in an environment of relative media stability. Now the host of electronically based, untested, computer-oriented information systems we call the new media threatens to change the basic structure of the communications industry. And that change is already taking place. Whether from fear of competition or hunger for profits, established media are increasingly hedging their communications bets and involving themselves in one or more new media enterprises.

Opportunities for Newspapers in New Media Ventures

The opportunities available to the established media participants venturing into new media waters are diverse. They include areas such as cable TV, electronic mail, electronic yellow pages, direct broadcast from satellite (DBS), multipoint distribution service (MDS), videotex and low-power television, among others.

An example of one opportunity newspapers might consider is DBS. Although the initial excitement over DBS has cooled, companies are considering launching powerful new satellites into orbit to beam a 12-gigahertz (Ghz) signal to earth. A dish the size of a trash can lid now receives TV signals directly at the home from transmitters 22,300 miles in space. One important use for this new medium is transmission of computer software and information.

While newspapers might conceivably become information providers for DBS transmissions, they could also be affected by DBS on another front. The FCC has ordered newspapers to stop using the 12-Ghz frequency for transmitting newspaper pages to their remote printing plants to make way for DBS. The mandate could have a significant economic impact on newspapers.

As is evident from the discussion above, DBS is but one of the many new media systems that are having an impact on journalism. The frenetic, experimental phase of thse new information systems has been characterized as a solution looking for a problem. A technological system searching for a problem to solve, or a market to serve, is expensive. Consider INTELPOST, the U.S. Postal Service project that began in 1978 as a means of sending electronic messages overseas by satellite. Six years of development and testing ran up a bill of $6.2 million. Yet at a cost of $5 per page to the sender, gross revenues totaled less than $60,000 by 1983—about one percent of costs.[14] A House Government Operations subcommittee reported that " There is little reason to believe that revenues will even come close to matching current expenditures in the near future, let alone recover past costs."[15]

The influence of the new media on journalistic institutions is all the more curious considering money-losing efforts such as INTELPOST.

Local Newspaper Involvement

How fast is new media development occurring? Before 1980 only a handful of newspapers were involved in electronic transmission and display of text information to the home. By 1981, according to the American Newspaper Publishers Association, 69 U.S. newspapers had arranged to provide some sort of local cable programming. In April 1983 the ANPA published a survey of nearly 1050 U.S. and Canadian dailies, asking, "Are you considering, planning, participating in, or operating any kind of cable, teletext, videotext, or low-power TV venture?" Forty-eight percent responded affirmatively. Ninety percent of newspapers with circulations over 500,000 answered yes. Yet those newspapers with less than 5000 circulation, despite the high costs involved, also had high involvement: 41 out of 98 answered affirmatively.[16]

The involvement of the small newspaper chains and independents is significant.[17] An important question is how newspapers will preserve their community orientation against competition from larger communications companies. To the extent that the new media are not as limited by the old media boundaries of time and space, giant companies, such as American Telephone and Telegraph (AT&T) and CBS Inc., could tend to monopolize communications. But new media exploration by small daily and weekly newspapers indicates that the community market remains a vital and independent one for them.

Financial investment in the new media on the part of a local newspaper is controversial, however. It means fewer resources for the rest of the newspaper. It could mean fewer reporters, or a year's delay in expanding the press. Many devoted journalists are angry about management spending time and money on electronic publishing because they see it as foreign to their business and a threat to their own jobs.

Management often has difficulty defending its explorations because they are just that . . . ventures into the unknown. It is hard to say what the long-term rewards will be, while the expenditures in the short run are obvious. Rewards and expenditures notwithstanding, management must deal with the effects of these new ventures on current operations and employees.

Reactions to the Changing Nature of Journalism

As we have already seen to some extent, journalism's strategic planners, faced with rising costs of labor and newsprint, have embarked on a bold exploration of the new media, as they believe these technologies will give them a tool with which to compete with television and radio. Despite the uncertainty about the eventual importance of any one of the new media, journalism planners continue to investigate equipment options, to complete FCC forms and to plan for the future.

These new media are accompanied by many new and challenging ideas about how to gather, store, process and deliver information, and, at the same time that they are branching out into the new fields, newspapers are using these newly learned concepts to restructure internal operations as well. Indeed, one aspect of this situation that has often been overlooked is the internal, corporate impact on communications businesses. Journalism, after all, is a tradition-steeped business.

One journalist, Garrett Ray, warns that the day may come when no one will be left to remember "the clatter of a Model 14 Linotype in a country newspaper shop."[18] Thus, it seems that while corporations that bear the proud names of Hearst, Pulitzer and Gannett talk excitedly about the information business, many of their front-line journalists do not. A gap has emerged between management and staff over the new technology. If the challenges of the new communications environment described in this book are to be met, this gap must be quickly bridged.

Journalists tend to see their calling in strict terms of truth and falsehood, unchanged by war or riot, by invention or economics. But journalism, as a profession and as a set of standards, has never been independent of the tools used to communicate a given message. The changes required by the new media and the evolving communications environment are no exception, and it is evident that they *will* come. Whether their impact is felt mostly in the 1980s or in the 1990s is irrelevant because they must be anticipated and confronted now.

According to Katharine Graham, "The competition newspapers face in the media marketplace of the 1980's is already tougher than it has ever been previously—and with videotext and teletext and Direct Broadcast Satellites just over the horizon, the situation we face is only going to become more complex in the 1990's."[19]

Others believe the challenge is already fully upon us. Says Michigan newspaper publisher Phillip Power:

> It seems to me that the central issue that we've got to face as [...news-paper entrepreneurs,] is how to drive our organization through the transition between being newspaper companies and being communication companies or information companies. And I think the reason for that point is fairly obvious, if you consider the fact that we're now in the middle of the communications revolution which is characterized by linking digitized databases on computers, to a telephone or other switching system, to terminals ... we have the most significant social and economic phenomenon taking place now, since the industrial revolution, period. And if we don't understand it, and we don't adapt to it, and we don't figure out what's going on, we're going to wind up on the ash can of history.[20]

Not all newspaper industry participants may share these views. However, almost all agree that the pressure of the new media does necessitate some change in the way newspapers conduct business. The new media were first and foremost seen as a threat—a view that still tends to color any discussion of them today. Whether they emerge as a threat or asset to the newspaper of the future, it is more than likely that the newspaper of the future *will* change. As Dr. F. W. Burkhardt commented:

> Our children will be taught over terminals, friends will send us screen messages, our living-rooms will be designed around a TV communication center. We will have home robots (which you can even buy today in Silicon Valley for slightly over $500). They will sweep the *floor* and fetch the *slippers* and *pick up the newspaper* from the doorway. Do you believe that the newspaper will be just the same as it is today? I rather doubt it.[21]

ROLE OF NEWSPAPERS IN A TECHNOLOGICAL SOCIETY

The new media environment, where new forms of communications are quickly born, yet are only gradually understood and assimilated, is characterized by unpredictability. In a vast game of technological roulette—a game with billions of dollars at stake—nobody knows which media will serve which markets best. Newspapers, with their market experience and local presence, could be the key.

Newspapers must bring their profit-oriented approach to the question of how new systems can actually be applied. No business is better suited to sell new information products to the local market. Thus, newspapers can help assure that the new media will not continue to be a solution looking for a problem.

Moreover, newspapers can use their powerful research capabilities to help determine which services people really want and the best way to provide them.

One irony of the technological society is that the greater the short-term emphasis on technology, the scarcer and more valuable become the human inputs of creativity and production. For example, cable operators today find they have laid millions of dollars of coaxial plant, taking the signal from the uplink to the satellite transponder to the earth station, only to have the same old routine programming eventually reach the home. The overemphasis on *how to deliver* means that the pendulum will have to eventually swing back to the question of *what to deliver.* Newspapers are experts in what to deliver.

Newspapers also add much-needed local flavor to what would otherwise be distant information products. For companies competing to provide videotex to local markets, newspaper local news may become one attraction.

A final strength of newspapers, perhaps ultimately more significant than all the others combined, is that newspapers and newspaper companies have the cash to provide capital. Concerns about newspapers becoming "cash cows" to finance flashy high-tech ventures are legitimate. But it is important to point out that those ventures are increasingly related to the vitality of the basic newspaper business. It makes less and less sense to talk of developing print journalism products *instead of* broadcast or electronic products, as the two have begun to merge. Jim Welch, former editor of the *Salem (Oregon) Capital Journal,* writes:

> Will electronic publishing replace newspapers?
>
> There are two answers: Probably not, and it already has. Strangely enough, both of these may have some validity. Many observers think newspapers, on paper, will be around in some form for decades or centuries.
>
> But these same people note that there no longer is a meaningful amount of mechanical publishing. It's flat out electronic even when the end product is paper.[22]

This "electronification" of the newspaper has resulted from efforts to reduce costs. It is simpler to use electronic and photographic means of manipulating information; you do not have to pay linotype operators to perform the process mechanically. Media expert Ben Compaine writes: "The technology has brought newspapers into the electronic age, if not with the same immediacy as television or radio, then with many of their techniques for instantaneous and remote transmission of the news back to the waiting pressroom."[23]

Thus, investment in telecommunications technology is not as antagonistic to the newspaper's basic mission as might have seemed the case a generation ago. Some newspaper publishers will no doubt be distracted from their basic business by unworkable communications ventures. The marketplace will be quick to reprove such cases of infidelity, just as it will reprove those media managers who, in an era of rapid change, choose to do nothing.

Larry Kahaner writes in the *Washington Journalism Review*:

> There is a cliché that the new technology leaves newspapers behind. Not true. Newspapers are in a better position than others news organizations to exploit the new technology. Whether they do depends on the newspapers themselves.[24]

What newspapers will do has become a key question throughout the communications business. The problem is not technology. The problem is not the potential of cable or the latest ruling of the FCC. The real issue is, what will newspapers do to respond to a communications business subject to rapidly increasing changes? Will newspapers try to exploit and develop these changes, or will they hold back and merely react?

The opportunities in information today are so great, one might say that communications has become a new, upstart business. All bets are off. This is as true for established media as it is for telephone, computer and cable companies. Established media willing to confront and take up the challenge of the new media must learn new ways of thinking about media and journalism. The chapters that follow provide a context within which such thinking can be translated into action as well as guidelines for determining the direction such action should take.

NOTES

1. John Morton, "Circulation: A Household Number," *Washington Journalism Review* (June 1984): 17.

2. Robert Reed, "Falling 'Star' Bad Sign for Newspapers," *Advertising Age* (March 29, 1982): 1.

3. J. Kendrick Noble Jr., "Four Expert Views," *presstime* (January 1985): 38.

4. Ralph Lee Smith, *The Wired Nation* (New York: Harper & Row, Publishers, 1972), p. 98.

5. Ibid.

6. Alvin Toffler, *The Third Wave* (New York: Bantam Books Inc., 1981), p. 3.

7. Ibid., 255.

8. Mel Tinney, address to the Suburban Newspapers of America (SNA) Cable TV Seminar, Airlie, VA (October 21, 1981).

9. Steve Piacente, "Parting Words," *CableVision Magazine* (May 10, 1982).

10. Judee K. Burgoon, Michael Burgoon and Charles K. Atkin, "What Is News? Who Decides? And How?" (A preliminary report conducted for the American Society of Newspaper Editors, May 1982).

11. David Shaw, *Journalism Today: A Changing Press for a Changing America* (New York: Harper's College Press, 1977), p. 229.

12. Katharine Graham, "Graham: 'We Are Not Ready for the Obit Page,' " *Publishers' Auxiliary* (May 3, 1982): 3.

13. Sydney Gruson, "The New Competition," *Editor & Publisher* (May 22, 1982): 8.

14. "Electronic Mail Proves Flop for Postal Service," *Washington Post* (April 26, 1984): 17.

15. Ibid.

16. Kathleen Criner and Raymond B. Gallagher, "Newspaper Cable TV Services: Current Activities in Channel Leasing and Other Local Service Ventures" (A report by the ANPA, March 1982). Also see "Cablenews Roster Update," *Electronic Publisher* (September 2, 1983): 1. The roster listed 80 newspapers involved in local cable programming with a total subscriber base of one million. During early 1983, the ANPA and the Newspaper Advertising Bureau surveyed 1050 U.S and Canadian dailies, "Survey of Newspaper Involvement in New Telecommunications Modes," (July 1983).

17. Interestingly, ANPA's March 1982 report found that about two-thirds of the dailies involved had a circulation numbering less than 50,000, and the majority had less than 20,000. Two-thirds of the weeklies involved in the new media had circulation of less than 10,000. New Media involvement of newspapers was found to be split, roughly, between independent and group-owned newspapers.

18. Garrett Ray, "Love Song to a Linotype," *SCAN* (A monthly periodical of the Advertising Checking Bureau, Inc., vol. 30, no. 2): 3-4.

19. Katharine Graham, in an address to the New England Newspaper Association (February 18, 1982).

20. Phillip Power, in an address to the Suburban Newspapers of America (SNA) Cable TV Seminar, Airlie, VA (October 21, 1981).

21. Dr. F. W. Burkhardt, "Electronic Media—An Overview," *IFRA New Media Report* (10) (1984): 1-6.

22. Jim Welch, "Electronic Information Services Blossom Under Dialcom," *Production News* (June 1982): 55-56.

23. Benjamin M. Compaine, *The Newspaper Industry in the 1980s* (White Plains, NY: Knowledge Industry Publications, Inc., 1980), p. 208.

24. Larry Kahaner, "Parting Words," *CableVision Magazine* (January 11, 1982): 134.

2

The Advent of the New Media

CHARACTERISTICS OF THE NEW MEDIA

Considered together, the new media mean an explosion in the number of information sources, changing the market assumptions on which established media businesses are based.

Generally speaking, these are the common characteristics of the new media:

1. *Market*—The new media tend to have a local rather than regional market presence compared to the broadcast media. "Presence" means local information content, or some appeal to the local market. It could also mean marketing or billing handled locally.

2. *Centralized Control*—The paradox of computer-based media is that while they may have a local presence, they may be controlled from a central location hundreds or thousands of miles distant. Whether this will become commonplace is a major question. It could have a powerful impact on community journalism. Thus, the new media present a strange combination of local and national elements.

3. *Text Capability*—The new media can take electronically "printed" words and can format them on the TV screen or computer terminal at home. Like newspapers, the new media trade in words, but the words are instantly printed and are often keyed into electronic information systems that update information rapidly.

4. *New Media Applications*—Each new medium can be used in several ways. Cable TV, for example, can be used for movie services or for cable text. This means added complexity to the communications environment.

5. *Information Orientation*—The new media are more information-based than entertainment-based. This is due to their text capability and their capacity for information storage. Because the new media can collect and transmit tremendous amounts of data, *for the first time a medium can be electronic and can be a medium of detail.*

6. *Viewer Effects*—The new media can be defined by their effects on the viewer. As has been noted many times, new media tend to make the viewer an active rather than a passive consumer of information. The new media get the viewer out of the easy chair to input data, send messages or generally interact with the system. An unresolved question, however, is how many consumers actually want to select their own information mix, as they have largely relied on the friendly neighborhood editor to do that in the past.

7. *Market Effects*—The new media can also be recognized by their effects on the communications marketplace. They make the market far more pluralistic, increasing the number of information outlets and causing further specialization among media. They open new markets and tend to weaken the barriers of entry to others. New media audiences tend to be highly selective and highly segmented, giving rise to the question whether the new media can be called "mass media" at all.

8. *Instability*—The new media have made communications much more volatile. This fact of permanent change has become a reality for the communications business, as newspapers exploring new communications forms soon find out.

None of the new media perfectly matches all these characteristics, but overall, these eight traits describe their impact. This inpact has been profound, enough to threaten the dominance that newspapers have traditionally enjoyed as a mature industry. Although joint operating agreements and mergers have steadily reduced the head-to-head competition among major newspapers so that today only a few markets have two, the picture is not as stable as it might appear.

INROADS BY OTHER MEDIA

The newspapers' hold on media markets started to weaken about 50 years ago. Beginning in the 1930s, household penetration of newspapers began to decline. That is, the number of households was increasing faster than circulation. Moreover, information consumers gradually became accustomed to turning to radio, and later, to television for breaking news. Radio and television confronted newspaper publishers with a "fight 'em or join 'em" choice in some ways analagous to the problems now posed by the new media.

Ironically, the first radio news program was sponsored by a newspaper, the *Detroit News*. It was broadcast from the newspaper's building, on August 31, 1920, carrying news of the Michigan primary election. After that it carried news information each day. The *Detroit News* viewed radio as an effective promotional tool for newspapers, in much the same way that many newspapers are using the new media today.

In 1927, the ANPA's radio committee agreed that radio news could increase newspaper sales. According to the committee report, that year 48 newspapers owned stations, 69 sponsored programs and 97 gave news programs via the airwaves.

The Associated Press reacted differently. In 1924, it tried to restrict its election returns to newspaper publication. The AP fined the *Portland Oregonian* $100 for broadcasting AP reports. Still, an estimated 10 million people heard of Calvin Coolidge's victory on the radio.[1]

With the advent of television, combined with economic changes and urbanization, evening newspapers began to suffer. Many gradually went out of business. Yet industry-wide, suburban dailies and weeklies grew, many of them dominating the advertising markets in their communities. For the majority of newspapers, the biggest competition came not from the local radio station and certainly not from the network broadcast affiliate many miles distant. The biggest concerns were shoppers, free-distribution publications and direct mail. In other words, other print competitors remained the newspaper industry's chief worry—through the 1970s.

This changed with the rapid expansion of cable television from the late 1970s through the early 1980s. Telecommunications became an increasingly common word at newspaper conventions. It seemed that publishers sensed that the newspaper's stable relationship with the community marketplace, which had weathered both radio and television, might no longer be inviolable.

For the publishers, used to checking profit figures casually at the end of the month, the realization of burgeoning communications paths to the hinterland was disturbing indeed. The fear of having their market shares gradually but greatly reduced by various new competitors motivated newspapers to act.

The key to this change was rapid development of several new media, some of which had existed in a less developed form for decades before emerging in the late 1970s and early 1980s.

Technological Developments

Reduced cost and size of consumer electronics made them available on a mass scale, with implications for the media. One example of rapid technological development was the personal computer, whose market hardly existed before the mid-1970s. Much of its development can be attributed to two whiz-kids working out of their homes: Steven Jobs and Stephen Wozniak. After work the two labored on a pet project—designing a small, easy-to-use computer. Jobs sold his Volkswagon bus to raise $1300 to start the business, the modest beginning of what became Apple Computer.

In 1979, 150,000 personal computers were sold in the United States. From there, the line jumps up to 350,000 in 1980, to half a million in 1981, to more than two million today. Four years after the sale of a Volkswagen bus, Apple Computer earned $200 million.[2]

Today more than 50 newspapers can be accessed in electronic format through personal computers or through computer terminals. But even this development may pale in significance beside the invention of video games. In 1972 Nolan Bushnell, a relatively unknown electronics inventor, parlayed a little-remembered video game called Pong into a video games company named Atari. Four years later, he sold the company to Warner Communications for $28 million. In 1981 Atari was the profit leader for Warner, with revenues of $200 million, although it has not fared as well since.[3]

Atari demonstrated the extraordinary amount of money to be made in computer-related entertainment. But perhaps more important, video games meant that an entire generation of American youngsters would grow up accustomed to manipulating computers and televisions. Children ventured behind the TV set, plugging terminals into video inputs and manipulating connectors as studio technicians do. This was a radical change from only a generation before, when warnings of radiation had made the television a welcome guest in the living room only it it could be kept at a certain distance. The turnabout in attitude makes it seem likely that future consumers will adapt to electronic innovation more quickly, forcing newspapers and other businesses to react more quickly as well.

Technological Trends

These examples—video games and the personal computer—illustrate two main trends and two derivative trends in telecommunications and electronics:

- *Reduced Price*—Once the high research and development costs have been recovered, the cost of actual production tends to go down. Examples include: personal computers, microprocessor chips, calculators, television cameras, Beta and VHS units and many others.

- *Reduced Size*—As technological innovation occurs, the units get increasingly portable. Today's consumer can watch television on a wrist TV, can listen to a radio in a sun visor, can play musical tunes from a watch, and so forth.

Mass availability and increased competition have resulted from these trends. Reduced price means consumers can buy new devices, which makes for a more lucrative market. This attracts many new competitors. Of course, this is a simplified picture. These factors are dynamic: size affects demand, demand affects price, price and demand affect competition, which in turn contributes to reduced price, and so forth.

The development of the mainframe computer illustrates these trends. A visitor to the IBM 360 mainframe Model 30, introduced in the early 1960s, would have been impressed by its specially air-conditioned room of at least 18 square feet. This space housed the central processing unit (CPU), the printer, a control console and a desk for a keypunch operator. The CPU itself was about five feet high and six feet wide. It was water-cooled to prevent overheating. At full speed, the 360 Model 30 could do 33,000 calculations a second. Its cost *in 1968 dollars* was $280,000.

The desktop personal computer introduced by IBM, the IBM PC, also has a CPU. It is contained on a silicon chip about the size of a fingernail. The entire computer fits on top of a desk and has a computational speed of 700,000 calculations a second. The fully equipped IBM PC costs less than $3000, meaning that communications devices that depend on complex calculations and circuitry are available to a mass market.

For newspapers, this innovation means that barriers of time and distance and economics that used to protect the home newspaper market from intrusion no longer exist. Whether telecommunications and computer companies can deliver a quality news product to local communities is open to debate. But they now clearly possess the technical capability to do so. That technical capability is what the new media are all about.

INVESTMENT OPPORTUNITIES

How this capability will affect the newspaper business is an open question. The answer depends on two factors: profit potential and newspaper relevance. Newspapers will be most attracted to media that appear to be financially feasible on the one hand and complementary to existing newspaper businesses on the other. A classic example of this formulation would be Dow Jones News Retrieval—an online database service targeted for business customers, created by the company that owns *The Wall Street Journal, Barron's* and the Dow Jones News Service.

Newspapers interested in exploring new communications will therefore view new media as: (1) financially feasible and highly adaptable to newspaper use; (2) financially feasible but not very adaptable; (3) financially speculative but very adaptable; or (4) financially speculative and not very adaptable.

It is important to point out that these are dynamic categories. Once a medium is seen as financially viable, competitors will gravitate toward it, possible making it less attractive to subsequent entrants. When Dow Jones made its move into electronic information in 1974, database publishing was a much more speculative venture. Similarly, technological evolution will change newspaper perceptions of how adaptable a medium might be to newspaper use. The spread of home computer terminals, for example, might make optical disk storage of information more financially viable and more adaptable to newspaper use. "Adaptable" in this context means the medium becomes more relevant to what newspapers are accustomed to doing: disseminating new information on a mass scale.

A newspaper company could move into a new media venture more because of compatibilities with its existing businesses than because of proven financial opportunities. In many respects, this is the soundest reason for it to invest in developing a new medium, given the latter's financially speculative nature. For a company like the *Dallas Morning News,* in the rare situation of a two-newspaper town, it makes sense to invest in a cable TV–leased channel if only for promotional reasons—aside from profit potential. Similarly, when Knight-Ridder began to market electronic storage services to the nation's newspapers, it knew that it wanted to store its own newspapers electronically anyway.

Thus we can lay out new media opportunities graphically. Figure II.1 portrays the relationship of new media to newspapers.

One could argue endlessly where exactly on the graph a given medium should go, and given the present rate of change in the new media, the picture would probably differ in six months anyway. But the conceptual framework has lasting importance, because any new-product manager will have to follow this analytical path to choose the best opportunities for the company to explore.

EXAMPLES OF THE NEW MEDIA

We shall consider each medium separately, keeping in mind that each has its own history and nature, and also that the list of new media here is probably incomplete and will grow in the future. Each medium has peculiar assets and weaknesses, each relies on unique hardware, and each offers special programming catering to a slightly different market.

These media are considered on a scale that measures their financial viability. However, any venture into a new communications form should be considered speculative, subject to high potential profit, high potential cost and a fluctuating technological environment.

Figure II.1: Relationship of New Media to Newspapers

RELEVANCE TO NEWSPAPERS

← MORE

LESS →

**ONLINE
DATABASES**

VIDEOTEXT

**OPTICAL
DISCS**

CATV

TELETEXT

**CELLULAR
RADIO**

LPTV   **MULTICHANNEL
MICROWAVE**

←— **FINANCIALLY
SPECULATIVE**   **ESTABLISHED** —→

CATV

Community antenna television (CATV), or cable television, is almost as old as television itself. Cable television development occurred in three phases. In the first phase, cable was basically ancillary to broadcast television, providing network television where broadcast signals could not reach. In 1975, the second phase began, with satellite communications and the rise of the satellite and premium channels. During this period, several established television programmers—including CBS, ABC and NBC—experimented with cable programming and found the segmented market too small for their liking, but nevertheless cable evolved from being a handmaiden of broadcast television to becoming a full-fledged competitor.

In the third phase, operators have begun to think of cable in broader terms. Some alternative possibilities they are now considering include: data transmission, text services, electronic classified ads, telephone service and transactions. Whether this kind of cable will become predominant is open to question.

Early CATV came into existence, in part, because hardware and appliance retailers wanted to sell TV sets to areas beyond the limited range of broadcast television signals. People on the wrong side of the mountain had poor reception, but by putting a tall antenna atop the mountain and using an amplifier to boost signal strength, one could drop an antenna cable over the ridge and supply reliable television service. Several homes were connected to a single, master antenna. The identity of the builder of the first community antenna system is much debated, but author Ralph Lee Smith credits Robert J. Tarlton of Lansford, Pennsylvania, who erected a community TV tower in 1949.[4]

Thus cable television began in rural regions of the nation, and the typical cable system during the 1950s and 1960s was small, rural and family-owned. It provided only off-air network and independent signals. In this respect, it was and is quite different from network television. Only recently has cable spread to large urban areas as its services have become more competitive with those of broadcast television. By the time controversial cable bids came to urban areas in the 1970s and 1980s, rural jurisdictions followed the political traumas with amusement—they had been successfully operating systems for decades. Cable television's rural roots would later stimulate the involvement of community newspapers in the so-called marriage of CATV and newspaper publishers in the early 1980s.

The development of communication satellites in the early-to-mid 1970s spurred the evolution of cable television. The satellites meant a single program could be beamed to cable systems throughout the country. Satellites hovered thousands of miles in space, receiving signals from one location and relaying them across the face of the United States. The rapid development of satellites paralleled that of electronics in general.[5] This gave cable systems programming that the networks did not have, as superstations and movie channels sprang up.

Once the cable operators had new fare to offer the TV audience, cable moved rapidly into major TV markets—New York, Dallas, Chicago, Boston and Washington, D.C.—and the penetration continues. The cost and difficulty of building these large cable systems are hard to appreciate. For example, the Fairfax County, Virginia, cable system, with more than 120 channels, could eventually cost more than $80 million to build. The franchise winner, Media General, will depend on profits from the *Richmond Times-Dispatch* and its other interests to help finance the system.

An important question is how realistic these bids turn out to be. Insufficient programming is a significant problem. Multiple channels divide up the audience into ever-tinier slices while production costs continue to rise. The average production cost for an hour of network television programming is more than $700,000—to produce a level of programming that many viewers now find unsatisfactory. If television programming is already weak, what good does it do to divide the weak programs among 60 or more cable TV channels?

One can hold out hope that programming will improve. If it does, the change will be the result of competition among programmers. Cable programmers may be forced to concentrate on reaching fragmented audiences through targeting special interests. CATV has been compared to magazine publishing in this regard, but the analogy fails to hold because of the cost of TV programming. The magazine model cannot be applied too well to cable. The reason: the economics of television production do not allow programmers to appeal to as many different audiences as magazines do. Not enough viewers watch to pay for the cost of the programming. In truth, cable shoots for an intermediate-range, or size, market—not a narrow one and not a mass one in the network sense.

Part of the problem is the undeveloped vocabulary in this territory. The new media are neither mass media nor "de-massified" media. They really are mid-media—they shoot for something in between.

How far can targeted programming—often called narrowcasting—be realistically extended? At some point audience numbers become ridiculously low from the advertiser's viewpoint. Advertising expert Leo Bogart comments:

> Inevitably, the cost efficiency of reaching tiny slivers of the population has to be less than the cost efficiency of placing messages before vast audiences. In addition, serious problems of measurement and evaluation occur when audiences are fractionated as they are in radio today and as they may be for television tomorrow. The advertiser can't be really sure of what he's getting.[6]

An example of these measurement problems is the void of cable audience statistics. According to Kathleen Criner and Jane Wilson of the ANPA, as of November 1984, only 6 of the 60 satellite cable TV services were tracked by A. C. Nielsen.[7]

Even as the cable programmers battle among themselves, however, their decisions are having an effect on the networks, as are videocassette recorders. In the first six weeks of the 1984-85 season, for example, the combined network viewing audience declined 2% to 3% from the same period the year before. David Poltrack, research chief for CBS, attributed the decline in part to cable and projected the network share to drop from 81% in 1983 to 70% by 1990.[8]

Putting aside the question of the viability of cable programming and the related question of the realism of contract franchises, we should note that these developments are generally working to the journalist's advantage. First, programmers seeking to appeal to segmented groups will find *information* a key part of the programming mix. The need for interesting information will gradually expand the role of journalism in CATV—a role that will grow much more quickly if cable succeeds.

Second, the franchises often call for local origination requirements that the cable company cannot fill. This creates a local programming void for some news organization. In 1984 Congress moved expressly to permit a news-paper to own a cable TV station within its circulation area. This merely tends to ratify existing FCC policy toward newspaper ownership—several news-papers are already cable operators within their markets. The *Lawrence Journal-World,* in Lawrence, Kansas, is owned by the same man who owns Sunflower Cablevision in that city, for example. But the law could eventually encourage major newspapers to buy nearby cable systems should they choose to do so, now that Congress has concurred with the FCC.

Despite the economic and even technological uncertainties in cable, it has already been established as a profitable business and therefore is the least speculative of the new media. Whether it will turn out to be more than entertainment is uncertain, however.

Because cable television is the oldest of the new media and the best estab-lished, it tends to overshadow the others. But it is useful to think of cable as part of a larger trend diversifying the communications scene.

Online Databases

The development of databases has depended on many historic trends, in-cluding but not limited to the reduced cost of computer terminals and personal computers, increased storage capacity of mainframe computers, software developments to allow simultaneous users, the general explosion in the level of society's information production, and the "electronification" of print-production processes using computer tapes for typesetting that could later be fed into electronic databases.[9] Lockheed Corporation, which owns Dialog Information Services, traces the development of databases back to 1962. That year it asked Dr. Roger Summit to begin exploring how the computer could be used to manage vast amounts of information. That effort received a shot in the arm in 1966, when NASA was struggling to organize the massive amounts of information generated by the effort to place a man on the moon. Lockheed, a step ahead in the field, won the contract to design the system. The NASA/RECON database resulted, and it created broader interest by other government agencies. In 1972, Lockheed introduced Dialog, offering information that could be called up onto a video display screen with the help of a computer terminal and a telephone.

The databases are important to publishers for two basic reasons. First, it gives them another way to repackage and sell their information. Many of the key players in the field are print publishers, including the publishers of *The Wall Street Journal* and *Reader's Digest.* Second, the online information systems are an invaluable and growing source of story material. While most of the systems are now used for fact-checking and background, the growth of census and business information could make the databases a primary source, at least for business reporters. The cost of using the systems can be high, however—anywhere from under $10 an hour to more than $100.

The online databases include Dow Jones News Retrieval, Nexis, Lexis, Dialog, The Source, CompuServe, Newsnet, Vu-Text and several others. These are the "database supermarkets," the vendors that collect many databases under one electronic roof. Dialog, for example, has more than 200 individual databases, ranging from ABI/Inform, a publisher of business abstracts owned by the *Louisville Courier Journal,* to *Zoological Record,* which covers zoological writings on an international level. The pool of publicly available databases is now estimated at more than 2000, and the number is growing at an estimated 20% to 30% annually.[10]

Several of the database companies, including Dialog, Dow Jones and Nexis, already say they are operating at a profit. Taking but a decade to establish profitability is a heady pace when it comes to new communications systems. Others, such as The Source, have fewer than 100,000 subscribers and have faced economic difficulty. But because of the large number of database publishers, investing here is relatively less speculative in the context of the new media.

Cellular Radio

Several companies, including the *Washington Post,* AT&T, GTE, MCI and others want to provide this service, which has been more than a decade in the making. As far back as 1970, the FCC tentatively allocated 84 megahertz of bandwidth for a new land-mobile telephone system. In 1971 Bell Telephone Laboratories submitted a proposal entitled "High-Capacity Mobile Telephone Service."

After 1974 the FCC granted several construction permits for experimental cellular radio systems. In 1980, encouraged by the results, the FCC issued "Notice of Inquiry and Proposed Rulemaking," and in June 1982 received petitions from companies interested in providing the service. The FCC plan allows for two cellular systems in each city—one to be operated by a traditional telephone company, called a "wireline" company by the FCC; and the other to be operated by a nonwire communications company ("nonwireline"), including newspapers. The prospect of newspaper competition with telephone companies is an interesting example of the "convergence of the modes" now affecting communications companies.

The concept of cellular radio—provision of mobile telephone communication—is similar to that of present car telephones. But mobile telephone systems currently have a limited range and can handle only a few simultaneous calls. In New York City, where there are more than 14 million registered automobiles, only a dozen mobile telephone calls can be handled simultaneously. This creates tremendous backlogs, and perhaps more important it limits the number of persons who can subscribe to the service. While 97% of U.S. residences have telephones, less than 0.1% percent of motor vehicles use mobile telephones. Only 700 mobile telephone units have been installed in New York City, with 1400 persons on a waiting list. By contrast, five-year projections estimate 250,000 subscribers to cellular-radio, car telephones there.[11]

Cellular radio addresses the problem of capacity by dividing each city into several cells, 2 to 10 miles in radius. Inside each cell is a two-way, low-power radio station. As vehicles move from cell to cell, the call is instantaneously "handed off" from one cell to another without interruption of service. By egg-crating a city in this fashion, the capacity of the system is greatly expanded, and many more calls can be handled simultaneously.

Cellular radio may soon make it possible to access databases while on the road; to obtain map displays, weather reports or traffic diagrams, even "stoplight news." But before any of this can happen, two major legal hurdles must be overcome, according to analyst Mark D. Schneider:

> First, nonwireline applicants for cellular licenses have challenged the FCC's decision to split allocation of cellular frequency markets between nonwireline applicants and wireline applicants. Second, nonwireline applicants have argued that wireline licensees should not be allowed to enter a market before its nonwireline competitors are licensed to serve in that market as well.[12]

Cellular radio systems are extremely expensive to build, costing tens of millions of dollars. Moreover, the cost of the service tends to restrict it to business users, although someday it may be affordable on a wider basis.

Most of the cellular systems are several years away from completion. But two factors are helping them along. One is the significant pent-up demand for mobile telephone service. Second is the impressive field of companies backing the development of the systems, including AT&T and some of the divested Bell operating companies.

Despite the apparent demand, the combination of high initial investment in a rapidly changing technological environment makes cellular radio at least somewhat speculative.

Optical Disk

Optical or compact disks are related to the videodisc pioneered unsuccessfully by RCA in the late 1970s and early 1980s, and also to Sony's audio disks, both introduced for entertainment purposes. But the real advantage of the disk may be information storage and retrieval rather than entertainment (or some combination of the two), because of its extraordinary capacity.

The optical disk holds from 500 to 1000 times more information than the floppy disks now used with personal computers. The name and address of every person in the United States could be recorded on a single 4.75-inch disk. "The entire works of the great artists of all time, encyclopaedias, dictionaries, travel guides—all these and much more can be stored on a very few discs."[13]

The optical disk, also called a "compact disk," works something like a phonograph. Information is recorded onto the disk by a tiny laser beam. The light pits the surface of the disk, whose tiny elevations can later be read, allowing the information to be recovered and converted into the binary system of "1" and "0" that computers understand.

Because optical disks can be called up individually or in sequence, the disks seem to combine the capability of television with that of books: one minute the frames move in motion-picture sequence; the next, frames appear individually, like the pages of a book. But present technology does not allow users to store information on the disk themselves—this can only be done with a laser device under controlled conditions. This may soon change, however.

Disk technology has already been tested. In 1981, Sears, Roebuck and Co. put its summer catalogue on videodisc format. Some car dealers are using disks as a sales and training tool. But the disks have yet to be tested by the involved market trials used for videotex and teletext. On the other hand, word that IBM has bought 1.5 million of the disks has fueled conjecture about IBM's plans and the disk's future. The optical disk, which is an entirely new medium, will require years of development before its true potential is realized. The medium is promising, but speculative.

Teletext

The fortunes of new media often seem to fluctuate based on actions and reactions of large communications companies. Nowhere is this as apparent as with teletext. A few years ago, it was considered among the most promising new communications systems because of its ready adaptability to network television and because of its low cost to the consumer.

Much of that optimism has vanished. The rapid development of online services as a competitor is one factor. The problem of occasionally garbled transmission over cable lines is another. But most significant is the decision by Time Inc. to pull out of teletext after making a $25 million exploration effort. Whether teletext can fully recover from that blow to its credibility remains to be seen.

The origins of teletext go back to 1971, when a young British engineer named Sam Fedida helped to invent it. Fedida was interested in merging the computer and the television. He programmed information into blank spaces in the standard TV signal—essentially by using the black line that the viewer sees on the home TV screen when the vertical hold goes out of adjustment. This space, called the "vertical blanking interval," can be programmed with information. A decoder in the viewer's home can summon the information to the screen. News, sports, weather and other information appear at the viewer's command. The number of pages available for recall can vary from 100 to thousands, depending on the mode of transmission and the time it takes for the page to appear. Teletext seems interactive, but actually is not.

Teletext could have an important impact on local journalism because it gives the networks a means of programming text information anywhere their signals reach. Of course, the spread of teletext, if it widens at all, can take place only as fast as the increased use of the decoders that it requires. But teletext is a further evidence that "local news market" is no longer synonymous with "exclusive news market."

The future of teletext is speculative. Arlen Communications has predicted that 20 million U.S. homes will have access to teletext by 1990. This would mirror the success of teletext abroad, particularly in the United Kingdom, where it has proved more viable than videotex. The present relevance of teletext to newspapers is probably more symbolic than anything else.

Videotex

Just as people could not agree how to spell the name of this system, nobody has quite figured out how to market it. Britain's Prestel system, for example, suffered a misguided early marketing effort and has never served the purpose for which it was intended: to increase usage of that country's telephone lines during off-peak hours. Videotex, which combines the text elements of online databases with sophisticated graphics and color capability, has mostly been restricted to tests in the U.S. Perhaps that is why it is hard for us to realize that videotex has been given every opportunity for success for more than a decade now in Britain. From an international perspective, videotex is not the brand-new technology it might appear to be.

CBS and AT&T have a videotex trial under way, called Venture One, located in Ridgewood, New Jersey, but the major market test of videotex in America does not appear to be going well: Knight-Ridder's Viewtron. The company, working with AT&T to provide the service in Miami, attracted only about 3000 subscribers its first year of operation compared to its target of 4500. One often-criticized aspect of the home information service is the AT&T SCEPTRE terminal it requires, which costs subscribers $600 to buy or $39.95 a month to rent. Although Knight-Ridder officials continue to express big hopes for Viewtron, the company dismissed 20% of its staff in October 1984. John Morton, a newspaper analyst for Lynch, Jones & Ryan, said of Knight-Ridder, "They're on the leading edge of a not very big business." But he added: "Ten years from now this could be a very big business and even competitive with newspapers. It behooves a newspaper company to be in the business."[14]

Videotex has been accused of being a solution in search of a problem. But we should be patient before calling a new medium a success or a failure. Many communications analysts would have been surprised had Viewtron achieved early success, because of the resistance to the high initial cost for a service most people knew nothing about.

Videotex has yet to demonstrate that graphics and color add enough value to compete successfully with online services. For this reason, videotex investment must be considered speculative.

Multichannel Microwave

In May 1983, the FCC authorized another new media service, multiple-channel microwave. The excitement generated by the FCC move is described by the ANPA:

> On Friday, September 9, 1983, the corridors of the FCC were jammed with messengers, clerks and attorneys carrying stacks and cartons of government forms. By the close of business, more than 1600 license applications were on file for multi-channel MDS, the newest video distribution service authorized by the Commission.[15]

MDS, a microwave-frequency TV service that often offers movies, has been available for years. But it offers only one channel. Multichannel microwave allows the broadcast of four MDS-type channels simultaneously. Thus a multichannel programmer could broadcast a sports channel, a national news channel, a movie channel and a local origination channel. The added channels mean the service is more competitive with broadcast television and other television services. Moreover, it can offer journalists an important third option for local coverage, the other two being cable and low-power television.

A complication for extablished media companies interested in multichannel is the FCC's regulation, thus far, of microwave as a common carrier, similar to telephone companies. That means the system owner cannot control program content. Newspapers want to control the information provided by their system. That makes them wonder how close they want to get to multichannel microwave, for fear that FCC regulation might seep over into First Amendment issues. (This concern is also voiced about cable.)

The solution seems to be to persuade a common-carrier company to build and own the transmission system. The newspaper can then enter into a long-term lease for program time, thereby maintaining control over content. The common-carrier company, as such, would have no influence over what the newspaper's channel would carry. Lease rates are set by the FCC.

The problem facing multichannel is competition. Consumers will be able to get video programming in many ways in the years ahead—why should they choose a system limited to 4 (or 8 or 16) channels? Until multichannel microwave finds something to offer beyond sports and movies, the investment has to be considered speculative.

LPTV

Low-power television (LPTV) represents the latest attempt by the FCC to diversify media control through fuller use of the broadcast spectrum. LPTV was created in 1979 by the direction of then-FCC Commissioner Charles D. Ferris. The concept: allow small television stations to broadcast television signals at low-power levels that will not interfere with larger television stations.

As with cable, low-power television technology has been around in a more basic form for decades. Once called a television translator station, it is still used in some parts of the country. The translator is another solution to the problem that led to CATV—poor rural television reception. The translator picks up the network signal and then rebroadcasts it with amplification over the airwaves instead of by cable. Within 10 to 30 miles of the translator station, the signal is strong.

LPTV uses electronic equipment similar to that employed by television translators, except that LPTV stations can also originate their own programming.

The potential for local coverage has excited publisher interest, especially among those tired of wrangling with uncooperative cable operators. As of this writing, LPTV is authorized to operate up to 100 watts in the VHF range and 1000 watts UHF, with a range of up to 30 miles depending on terrain, antenna height, signal pattern, receiving antenna and other factors.

The FCC, in awarding LPTV licenses, gives preference to minority-owned and nonmedia companies. Weekly newspapers also have an advantage. Christopher H. Sterling has written that LPTV could be "something of an experiment for a true marketplace environment," becuase of these ownership rules:

> Existing local radio and television stations were to be allowed to own an LPTV facility; networks could own LPTVs (though the original proposed rule-making had projected a ban here); there was to be no limit on either regional or national multiple ownership; and cross-ownership between low-power television and cable stations or newspapers was to be allowed.[16]

LPTV has been an important boost to the community television phenomenon sweeping the country. Some believe LPTV will fulfill its established purpose of extending a television voice to under-represented interest groups and minorities. David Armstrong, author of *A Trumpet to Arms; Alternative Media in America,* writes somewhat optimistically: "Low-power television should increase access to the airwaves by minorities, women, left activists, environmentalists, workers, and other elements of the broad, loose coalition of the disenfranchised that has, of necessity, invented alternative media."[17]

Whether LPTV will become a significant communications force is hard to predict, and its survival and profitability are uncertain. LPTV has limitations, chiefly short range and small audience. It has the same problem of limited channel capacity faced by multichannel microwave. Perhaps these limitations can be overcome with a network of LPTV stations. In any case, the more than 12,000 LPTV applications filed with the FCC since the 1982 report and order that created the service are a sign that the service is taken quite seriously by many. LPTV is another indication that the communications environment is growing more complex.

DBS

We have seen that the term "new media" can be somewhat misleading, because while it is accurate from the consumer's point of view, many of the services have existed in some more primitive form for decades. Direct broadcast from satellite is a brand-new service, however. The FCC began accepting applications for licenses in 1982. DBS was authorized despite misgivings voiced by the FCC that it might hurt the local programming efforts to be subsidized through movie-subscription revenues.

Operating at a 12- to 13-gigahertz frequency range, DBS satellites beam television signals directly from space to the home. Homeowners purchase their miniature earth stations, about three feet in diameter, to receive TV signals from 22,300 miles away.

In August 1982, a joint venture led by General Instrument Corp. and United States Communications, Inc., leased 10 transponders on Canada's ANIK-C2 satellite. Today United Satellite offers a DBS service, with four channels of programming for about $30 a month. Because the signal is medium-power, not high-power DBS, the receiving dish must be bigger—about four feet in diameter. USCI officials predict 3.75 million subscribers by the end of 1987.[18]

Combined with nationwide billing and collections, DBS could be a serious block to LPTV development. There has been some speculation that it could even compete with cable, although it has fewer channels. However, the initial interest in DBS has cooled substantially, due to the hundreds of millions of dollars in start-up costs. In August 1984, three companies notified the FCC they were withdrawing their applications for DBS: RCA American Communications, Inc.; CBS Inc.; and Western Union Telegraph. Five other companies, however, informed FCC officials that they plan to proceed with DBS service.

This reluctance to spend such tremendous amounts of money for a service that will probably serve only rural, noncable areas is understandable. But it would be imprudent to ignore a new nationwide communications system just a few years old. It would also be imprudent to view DBS investment as anything but speculative.

BROAD IMPACT

These, then, are the new media, and probably more examples will soon be added to the list. They combine to make the communications environment far more diverse, and much more volatile, than ever before. As with any new communications device preceding the new media—television, radio, direct mail—they are uncertain, speculative businesses in their early stages. Yet one or more of them will probably emerge in the future to be as powerful as television is today.

In addition, each of the new media has several applications. Cable, for example, provides 24-hour news, subscription movie services and text channels. Thus we cannot understand the explosion of communications diversity just by counting the number of new media. We must also consider the many different uses to which each can be put.

The impact of the new media is already being felt, and by no means are newspapers the most affected. As mentioned earlier, the networks are suffering audience decline—by about six prime time ratings points from 1980 through 1984. While a slippage of 2.3 points does not sound like much, each ratings point has traditionally translated into about $70 million in advertising income. It would appear that demassification, as Toffler calls it, is having its first effects. But CBS analyst Poltrack believes the impact of Cable is leveling off.[19]

Nor is cable television the real problem facing the established media. If it were, the solution might be to wait for cable to be superseded by some other technological innovation.

For newspapers and the rest of the established media, the challenge in the latter part of the 20th century has been, How do we deal with increasingly rapid change in communications technology? The established media before the 1980s responded with "the least ingenious solution," whatever modification required the least alteration in their standard outlook or procedures. Accordingly, newspapers leased cable channels to provide cable text; networks leased transponders to experiment with new sorts of television progamming.

The established media are beginning to resist the temptation of responding according to the Law of the Least Ingenious Solution. According to John Naisbitt:

> Now, more than 100 years after the creation of the first data communications devices, we stand at the threshold of a mammoth communications revolution. The combined technologies of the telephone, computer, and television have merged into an integrated information and communication system that transmits data and permits instantaneous interactions between persons and computers. As our transportation network carried the products of industrialization in the past, so too will this emerging communications network carry the new products of the information society.[20]

Local Impact

One of the unique aspects of this emerging communications network will be its community impact. Already we see people partially defining their communities by the communications services they receive: our system has 120 channels, yours has 60. The new media have their impact in the community because they enjoy the capacity to tailor information to the locality—even when they are national systems. This is a unique equation in the communications business, in which it has always been:

$$Mass\ Media = Mass\ Message$$

Now the equation is beginning to read:

Noncomputer-Based Mass Media	=	Mass Message, but
Computer-Based Mass Media	=	Mass Message, or
		Regional Message, or
		Viewer-Specific Message

Because our established media have generally relied on delivering what could be called a "lowest common denominator" message to whatever audience they served, it does not seem too farfetched to speculate that computer-based media could lead to a new kind of journalism, a journalism of the new media.

Consider the new-media journalism implications, for example, of The Weather Channel, owned by Landmark Communications, Inc. The Weather Channel takes regional weather updates from throughout the country and broadcasts the information nationwide. Cable operators in each region are given a decoder, so that only the weather bulletin for their region would appear on the home TV screen in text. (This is in addition, of course, to the video picture of a person reporting the national weather.) Landmark then equips the cable operators with computerized weather-sensing devices that constantly monitor and report the weather conditions outside the local studio. This local information is occasionally inserted into The Weather Channel in text form, thus offering a seamless mix of national, regional and local information.

Moreover, this system and others like it take information once considered strictly provincial and distribute it independently of the businesses that have traditionally provided it to the community—the local newspaper and the local radio station. The local information provider (IP) has been bypassed.

Serving the Community

The question arises whether the regional identity of markets could change as this networking increases. Leo Bogart, for one, argues persuasively that newspapers will remain particularly well suited to serve their local markets:

Local markets are changing shape under the pressures of urban change. Forty-four percent of all advertising is now local rather than national, up from 39 percent in 1960. Although Americans everywhere share the same network television and the same brands of soap, soup and corn flakes, their communities continue to be different in character and in shape and volume of consumer preferences.

Among the local media, newspapers are the peculiar embodiment of these differences, and the health of newspapers can be no better than that of the communities whose names they carry.[21]

To the extent that community identity is bolstered by community-targeted media, newspapers could find themselves strengthened. But what will happen when local media are owned and operated regionally or nationally, as is now possible? It does seem likely that readers' concepts of what constitutes news will change, as information from new areas reaches the home in new ways.[22] But there is no reason that well-managed local information providers cannot successfully adjust their content and continue to be that "peculiar embodiment" that Bogart speaks of. Indeed, a strong argument can be made that if local media accept new media tools, they will serve their communities even better than before. The path of future communications is a broad one.[23]

Newspapers are struggling to capitalize on a communications environment that is changing drastically. Electronics technology is advancing at a blistering pace, and newspapers are adapting, mainly by applying relatively well-known technologies to existing operations: electronic pagination and video display terminals, for example. But these internal changes give but a hint of the whirlwind of change roaring outside, as the viewer-reader changes from a passive to an active participant in the communications process.

How will newspapers, the wise old leaders of the established media, fare in the mercurial environment? Do they risk having their advertising shares gradually reduced by competitors from outside the community? To the contrary, evidence shows that newspapers are readying for the challenges that await them.

NOTES

1. Edwin Emery, *The Press and America* (Englewood Cliffs, NJ: Prentice-Hall, Inc., 1972), pp. 589–93.

2. "To Each His Own Computer," *Newsweek* (February 22, 1982): 44–45. Also see "Striking It Rich," *Time* (February 15, 1982): 36–40.

3. Ibid. Warner Communications Inc. sold Atari Inc. in June 1984 for $75 million plus $240 million in notes. Warner projected a $425 million loss for the second quarter of the year, largely because of a write-off of Atari losses. See "Atari Sale: Massive Change Ahead?" *USA Today* (July 3, 1984): 18.

4. Ralph Lee Smith, *The Wired Nation* (New York: Harper & Row Publishers, 1972), p. 3.

5. Consider, for example, the first commercial communications satellite, launched in 1962. AT&T Telstar 1 transmitted one TV signal—approximately twelve telephone calls at a time—about 875,000 bits of computer information a second. Yet twenty years later, AT&T would be readying Telstar 3, which would carry up to 1.4 billion bits of information a second. In inflated 1982 dollars, a Telstar 3 would cost about $8 million less than Telstar 1 cost in 1962. See "A Call Heard Round the World," *Washington Post* (July 11, 1982).

6. Leo Bogart, "Media and a Changing America," *Advertising Age* (March 29, 1982): 52–54.

7. Kathleen Criner and Jane Wilson, "New-technology Players Jockey for Position," *presstime* (November 1984): 23–25.

8. David F. Poltrack, "The Road to 1990: Half-Way Home," (CBS/Broadcast Group report available from CBS Inc., October 1985): 2–14.

9. Ithiel de Sola Pool, *The Technologies of Freedom* (Cambridge, MA: Belknap Press, 1983), pp. 28–40.

10. Tim Miller, "The Database as Reportorial Resource," *Editor & Publisher* (April 28, 1984): 70–104. Also see Larry Kahaner, "Hello Sweetheart, Forget Rewrite, GET ME THE COMPUTER!" *Washington Journalism Review* (December 1981): 16–21.

11. Mark D. Schneider, "Cellular Communications Service: Wireline Delivery or Delay?" *The Georgetown Law Journal* (1984, vol. 72), pp. 1183–1209.

12. Ibid, p. 1184.

13. Ronald B. Kaatz, *Cable: An Advertiser's Guide to the New Electronic Media* (Chicago: Crain Books, 1982), pp. 23–24.

14. John Morton, "Knight-Ridder to Fire 20% of Viewtron Staff: Poor Sales Are Cited," *Wall Street Journal* (October 31, 1984): 2.

15. Kathleen Criner and Jane Wilson, "Telecommunications: A Review and Update," (A presentation to the ANPA Telecommunications Committee, October 5, 1983): 4.

16. Christopher H. Sterling, "Television and Radio Broadcasting," in *Who Owns the Media,* by Benjamin M. Compaine et al (White Plains, NY: Knowledge Industry Publications, Inc., 1982), p. 344.

17. David Armstrong, *A Trumpet to Arms, Alternative Media in America* (Boston, MA: South End Press, 1981), p. 340.

18. Bernie Whalen, "DBS Firms to 'Dish Out' Video Programs to Millions of Homes," *Marketing News* (vol. 17, no. 24, November 25, 1983): 1–8.

19. David F. Poltrack, "The Road to 1990: Half-Way Home," (CBS/Broadcast Group report available from CBS Inc., October 1985): 4–6.

20. John Naisbitt, *Megatrends* (New York: Warner Books, Inc., 1982), pp. 23–24.

21. Leo Bogart, "Media and a Changing America," *Advertising Age* (March 29, 1982): 52–54.

22. Consider the 1982 pro baseball playoffs. More than 15 million cable television subscribers could follow the ups and downs of the Atlanta Braves on Ted Turner's WTBS, the Atlanta superstation. Newspapers across the country covered the phenomenon of local fans rooting for the Braves, the club that came to be called "America's Team." Thousands of fans from towns across the U.S. went to Atlanta to watch their "home team" play.

23. It is important to observe the term *new media* is not itself new. The idea of an information environment was addressed by John McHale, *The Changing Information Environment* (Boulder, CO: Westview Press, Inc., 1976). Also see Barry N. Schwartz, ed., *Human Connection and the New Media* (Englewood Cliffs, NJ: Prentice-Hall, Inc., 1973). He uses the term to refer to satellite communications, videotape, electronic high-speed printing and holography as forms of New Media.

3

The Newspaper–Cable Marriage

By the 1980s, scores of newspaper companies were buying into cable television. Newspapers, more aware of cable than of the other new media, were anxious to get involved in new forms of communications coming to their communities. But the fear of competition, rather than community spirit, motivated them. They were worried that other communications media might steal advertising dollars away.

Yet during the first half of the decade, newspaper advertising revenue enjoyed healthy increases of about 12% a year. Revenue growth in 1984 was even stronger, about 14%. Newspapers continued to enjoy the largest advertising market share of any media, about 22% to 24%, and more than 62 million Americans still purchased a daily newspaper each day.

Underlying the sanguine statistics, however, were signs of vulnerability. The first indication was that revenue gains primarily reflected rate hikes rather than increased business.[1] There was a limit to how high the rates could realistically go. The actual ad linage, or volume of business, for the three major categories of ads—national, retail and classified—only expanded a few percentage points a year. Nor could the higher rates be justified by greater circulation, which had been flat for more than a decade.

Tired of watching rates climb faster than circulation, major advertisers began to consider alternatives to newspapers. For example, a marketing executive for Sears, Roebuck and Co., David W. Slowthrower, told a newspaper group, "Take a good hard look at your insertion rates, we certainly are. Are you fully aware of the competition in your market?"[2]

A second warning signal for newspapers was the growth of direct mail. Of special concern was "marriage" or shared-mail advertising, wherein several companies combined their advertising in one envelope to save money. For example, K-Mart and other advertisers knew that newspaper circulation was growing slower than the growth in total U.S. homes. This meant declining household penetration. In response, K-Mart ceased its Los Angeles newspaper advertising in favor of direct mail, reaching more homes for less money.

A third trouble sign, particularly for urban papers, was the emergence of robust suburban newspapers. Thus an established newspaper sometimes found an upstart competing with it for ads. Analyst John Morton warned that big dailies had been paralyzed by what he termed their "old, arrogant daily-newspaper attitude."[3]

A fourth weakness: increased costs of doing business. Fuel and newsprint costs were rising steadily, until the price climb of those two important newspaper resources leveled off temporarily in 1984. There could be little doubt that soon these costs would begin to edge back up, probably faster than the general rate of inflation. One newsprint manufacturer estimated that newsprint demand would exceed North American supplies by some 300,000 tons in 1987. While excess newsprint production capacity in other countries might compensate, this would mean attenuated supply lines. The ANPA's manager for newsprint and transportation, Joseph F. Prendergast, Jr. said, "North American supply-demand figures indicate a real need for more capacity in the near future."[4]

Increased production costs meant that the print media became more expensive, and readers harder to come by. MIT's Research Program on Communications Policy examined this relationship between readership and cost. Covering the trend period from 1960 to 1978, the study found almost every form of paper-based communication increasing in cost, while newspaper popularity rose only slightly. In comparison, all forms of electronic communication steadily grew less expensive and more popular.[5]

Despite the rosy statistic on popularity, these factors spelled out more competition for newspapers.[6] The effect was easy to read on the most important scorecard of them all: the number of dailies that survive. Despite the strongest economic recovery since World War II, the number of daily newspapers in the United States decreased by 16 in 1983 and by 13 in 1984. J. Kendrick Noble, Jr., a newspaper analyst for Paine Webber Inc., said, "Newspapers that are second in their markets to strong leading dailies and evening newspapers likely will continue to fail as many have in the high interest-rate environment of the past decade." He projected a net decrease of 84 daily newspapers between 1985 and the end of the decade.[7]

Historically, newspapers have responded to economic pressure by streamlining operations. Replacing the old linotype machines (and operators) with VDTs and phototypesetting units is the classic example. But one analyst,

Thuman R. Pierce, Jr. of the J. Walter Thompson Company, has said that new tactics are now in order, "because in the 1980s, the cost-cutting technology will run out as a means of protecting your profit. You must find another way to increase your bottom line."[8]

John Morton agreed: "What these statistics boil down to is that, despite the handsome profits, newspapers have some underlying problems that need attention. The most serious is sluggish circulation growth, particularly in comparison with the growth in household formations."[9]

Abstract statistics could assume grim reality when newspapers closed and people had to look for new jobs. Editor Stephen D. Issacs experienced this when the *Minneapolis Star* merged with the *Tribune*. Issacs said, "I talked to many publishers recently, and was startled by the number who have in effect told me that the newspaper industry is a dying industry. A dinosaur. Some will survive—the very big and the very small—but the in-betweens are going to face rough times in this electronic era."[10]

This seriously vulnerable position in an increasingly competitive environment brought several responses.

NEWSPAPERS REACT

The most publicized response was newspaper flirtation with cable ownership. Companies that joined in the great cable buy-in included the *Washington Post,* Dow Jones & Co., Media General and many others. The often massive investments in cable systems and programming networks were somewhat controversial within the industry. For example, Dennis Holder, a Dallas free-lance writer, charged that publishers were "reacting to the perceived threat from cable with hysteria approaching panic." Only gradually did publishers realize there was no pot of gold at the end of the cable rainbow.[11]

Newspaper ventures into cable ownership were harmless and in some cases instructive. They served to increase newspaper awareness of a changing media environment. And the newspapers learned a few lessons about the problems of profitability in a new communications field.

Ownership was only the most obvious response, however. More subtle and important changes were also occurring. One was the increased willingness to lobby government officials on telecommunications issues that now no longer appeared irrelevant to newspapers. In the 1970s, many publishers had been wary of such lobbying. Katharine Graham discussed this "above the fray" stance:

> —Some of us still felt that since our newspapers report on the work-
> ing of government—and comment on the actions of government on
> our editorial pages—we really did not want to be in the position of
> going to the government and urging it to take specific actions . . .
> out of concern that some members of the government might come
> back to us and ask for specific stories or editorials in return.[12]

Communications businesses with an eye on newspaper advertising markets, such as AT&T, had no such qualms. In the new environment of the eighties, newspapers joined with cable companies in lobbying to keep a deregulated AT&T from providing information and advertising services over its monopoly-controlled lines. This fracas demonstrated the degree to which telecommunications and publishing markets were converging, and it highlighted the usefulness of newspaper advocacy. AT&T professed to the judge overseeing antitrust procedures that it had no interest in electronic publishing.[13] But it opposed rules that would bar it from that activity. "We don't want to be restricted," explained Howard J. Trienens, the vice president and general counsel of what was the world's largest company. "We want to be like everybody else."[14]

Similarly, the man who gained fame describing television as a vast cultural wasteland, former FCC Chairman Newton Minow, said, "The people in the cable business and the people in the newspaper business are taking a position which would say AT&T is a 'monopoly'—yet, most of the cities in this country, tragically, are one-newspaper towns, and there's a monopoly. Every cable system in the United States is a monopoly."

Newspaper spokesman Robert Marbut retorted: "I don't see the similarity at all between one communications company which covers most of the United States, and 1750 daily newspapers, 6000 weekly publications and the 20,000 other print publications that are available to people in this country."[15]

Bell eventually agreed not to offer information services over *its own lines* for at least seven years. But this left a loophole big enough for even Ma Bell to waltz through. After all, Bell was divesting itself of 22 local operating companies whose lines it would no longer own. In 1985, AT&T announced plans for a videotex service.

Thus newspapers could hardly claim victory in their AT&T skirmish. But they had committed themselves to the ongoing process of governmental lobbying, as the increasingly competitive environment required.

Competitive pressures also forced newspapers to upgrade existing newspaper operations. Some improvements went beyond the traditional cost-cutting moves: enhanced color registration, following the lead of the Gannett national newspaper, *USA Today;* satellite transmission of newspapers from one region to another, pioneered by *The Wall Street Journal;* development of nonpetroleum newspaper inks and continued research into pulp substitutes, such as kenaf; and a burgeoning use of information databases, such as Nexis, Dow Jones News Retrieval and Dialog, for fact checking, background and research. Such investments, uncharacteristically involving a value-added rather than a cost-saved dimension, indicated newspapers would seek to thrive rather than to merely survive.

Another response to competition was a greater commitment to newspaper-related research and development. Changes in the overall communications environment had caught newspapers unaware, and now newspapers were establishing research departments to keep that from recurring. For example, Gannett established a New Media Task Force that spun off of *USA Today* to offer two online data services. The ANPA's telecommunications department accelerated efforts to study technological advances. Similarly, many institutions of higher learning, including Brigham Young University and the University of Florida, established videotex or electronic publishing centers.[16] This meant corporate research was soon augmented by an academic research structure, perhaps stimulating more serious research efforts by the nation's journalism schools. For the first time, journalistic academicians would have an opportunity to earn greater respect from both the professional and the academic establishments.

The interest in cable ownership and the more subtle though more significant, moves toward lobbying, upgrading of existing operations and newspaper R&D were all responses to increased competition. The biggest competitive rival of newspapers over the years had been television. As a result, the newspaper-cable marriage began and newspapers started to offer local TV programming.

THE NEWSPAPER-CABLE MARRIAGE

Newspaper publisher Arthur W. Arundel, who leased a cable channel in Leesburg for Virginia's largest weekly, the *Loudoun Times-Mirror,* described the relationship this way: "It really is like a marriage. The cable company does what it does best; they string the cable and operate the system. The newspaper does what it does best, providing local news to the community."[17]

Not dependent on newspaper ownership of cable, these marriages usually began with a prenuptial contract called a "leased channel agreement." These spelled out the terms of the arrangement. Newspapers would program the channel and pay for the privilege with cable TV listings, advertising services, a flat monthly fee to the cable owner or payment of a percentage of revenues.

The agreements varied in length from 1 to 15 years. Cable operators tried to hold down the length of the obligation for reasons explained by Steven Effros of the Cable Antenna Television Association. He asked publishers whether they would sign a five-year contract with an advertiser for "page five." "Would you do it?" he asked. "Would you give away page five, give away editorial control, give away the whole ball of wax? . . . Of course you wouldn't. That's what you're asking the cable operator to do."[18]

Once the agreements were hammered out, the programming began. This programming usually took one of two forms, text channel or video. The text channels were the most basic, composed of computer-generated words produced at the cable studio and transmitted to the viewer's home. About 60 words fit on a screen or "page," and the pages were cycled automatically. The computers used to format the pages were called character generators, which had long been employed by broadcast television to put names and other printed information on the television screen. Today, a typical character generator may have 200 to 500 pages of memory and can display several different colors. The cost of the device ranges from $10,000 to $40,000. Once programmed, the character generator reads and transmits the pages in a continuous loop over the cable channel. Short news items, sports scores, weather and classified ads are typical character-generator fare.

The second form of newspaper TV programming involved video. Far different from standard broadcast programming, newspaper TV programming was more localized and far less polished, as a rule. Usually inexpensive studio and remote cameras were employed to do the job. Newspaper video might be offered in a newsbreak format, a half-hour news program each night or news documentaries. The expense of video production meant most newspaper video was on the air only a few hours a day. Public access programming, or cable text, would fill up the rest.

ORGANIZATIONAL STRUCTURE

The major question raised by newspaper-cable programming was how these efforts should be structured within the existing newspaper organization. Because the idea of a group of entrepreneurs working within the organization was new, these structures evolved differently, depending on the particular needs of the newspaper. But internal structure was an important matter, one that later influenced the development of more advanced newspaper forays into the new media.

Although there are few hard-and-fast rules to go by, an analysis of newspaper-cable structure reveals a spectrum, ranging from newspaper-dependent operations on the left to radically independent ones on the right.

The development of cable programming has been greatly affected by the degree of control exercised by newspaper traditionalists within the overall organization. Most operations have been a variation of one of three organizational models. Many newspapers have begun with one model, then moved to another as they gain experience and confidence with the undertaking. Many have begun with a newspaper-dependent venture, the Bureau Model.

The New Media Bureau

The Bureau Model is designed to be as nonthreatening to the newspaper as possible. Usually, all staff decisions made by the bureau—the hiring and firing—must be approved by one or more newspaper staff members. Newspaper staffers are reassured when they see that the new venture fits snugly under the wing of the mother newspaper.

Usually some connection between the newspaper sales staff and that of the upstart venture is maintained. After all, an independent sales force can be quite threatening when the newspaper ad staff is already under pressure to sell more ads. Often cable ads are sold only by the existing sales force, although these salespeople are unaccustomed to the medium.

On the editorial side, the cable staff enjoys limited independent news-gathering authority. Its rewrites of editorial department copy must be reviewed by the newspaper editor or a designate.

As for entrepreneurialism, the exploration of new business directions is discouraged. The cable staff is there for a specific reason: to promote the newspaper via cable. Its main job is programming.

Usually cable text fits best into this model. It is relatively inexpensive and provides an insurance policy of sorts, should cable begin to challenge the newspaper's viability. An underlying assumption, however, is that cable (and later, the other new media) requires no substantial modification of existing newspaper strategy. Partial measures will do. Or, alternatively, it reflects the view that existing staff must be gradually and carefully co-opted to avoid conflict.

The advantage of the Bureau Model is that it causes minimum disruption of existing operations. But its usefulness is limited.

The Cooperational Model

The second model, toward the middle of the hypothetical spectrum, is the Cooperational Model. This calls for close cooperation between newspaper and cable staffs. While the two may not be equally important, they can work independently. The executive of the cable channel probably reports to a general manager, vice president or other officer of the corporation at large. While the cable staff may not initially sell its own advertising, it must eventually become self-supporting and more than a PR tool.

Along with the added responsibility comes an independent sales and news force. The cable staff selects, edits and gives the news, which may or may not come from the newspaper newsroom. The cable operation fully competes with other newspaper departments for resource allocation. Usually its responsibilities go beyond running the text channel.

There are underlying assumptions involved in the Cooperational Model, which is meant to prepare the organization for other changes as well as cable and to instruct it about the new communications environment. The new media group, in addition to providing cable TV programming, performs research and development tasks, conducts surveys and the like.

An example of the Cooperational Model is the Eau Claire Press Company's "Tele-Leader" cable venture in Eau-Claire, Wisconsin. Although the publisher of the *Leader-Telegram* initially tried to use newspaper salespeople for cable projects, eventually the need for an independent sales force was recognized. The publisher hired its own ad staff and management team to program the channel, realizing that cable television required a different sales pitch.

The independence can cause rivalry with established newspaper departments, and here the model gets tricky. For it to succeed, newspaper and cable personnel should work together. The best way to achieve this is through open management. Inevitably, the fear that the newspaper faces competition from the cable team surfaces. But friendly competition is fine as long as the overall goals of the organization are achieved.

Dissension is the risk of the Cooperational Model. The advantage is that it involves people from the established media in planning, news and advertising without impairing development. This makes traditional staffers approach future change more flexibly than would otherwise be the case.

Church and State

Given the problems of the Cooperational Model, some publishers opt for the Church and State Model. This model isolates the new media venture from the established media organization either because its members might adapt poorly, or because it wants to maintain a high degree of creative, independent control.

Donald F. Wright, president of the *Los Angeles Times,* has commented on why cable and other entrepreneurial efforts might require this type of treatment. Today's newspapers, he said, must respond to the marketplace as

entrepreneurs, and cannot simply draw on the experiences of other newspapers when deciding what to do:

> Many of us could fall into the trap of trying to manage our entry
> into the electronic field with an effort that is under-funded, under-
> staffed and managed by people without experience as entrepreneurs.
> There's a lot to be said for establishing a separate group of people,
> adequately funded, with the single objective of developing a new line
> of business.[19]

Such sentiments have led to the Church and State Model of organization,
in which the newspaper and the cable channel are separate enterprises owned
by the same company, including part or all of the cable system. As far as
management is concerned, the less they have to do with one another the
better. Often the cable venture is separately incorporated. It may be located
in its own plant. The staff of the new media enterprise will rarely consult
newspaper staffers. While they may keep an eye on communications developments, they are mainly concerned with how these will affect their enterprise.

One example of the model is Sunflower Cablevision of Lawrence, Kansas,
owned by Dolph Simons, publisher of the *Lawrence Journal-World*. The
system was built in the early 1970s. By 1981, more than 11,000 subscribers
were connected to the 15-channel system.[20] And, according to manager Dave
Clark, that figure now stands at more than 15,000 subscribers.

Simons separated cable from his paper to avoid cross-ownership and
conflict-of-interest charges. The cable plant is located down the block and
across the street from the newspaper. It has separate management and its own
resources.

The advantage of the Church and State Model is that it gives the corporation a free hand. The Corporation does not have to answer to traditionalist
forces. A company might also adopt this plan to limit its liability, to reduce
staff resistance, or to lessen fears of labor disputes over the reuse of newsroom news.

These, then, are the three organizational models that have been used for
cable. Each has had its own advantages. Actual ventures have rarely followed
a given model in all respects, often evolving from one model to the next in
response to profitability problems. Publisher Phillip Power of Michigan has
observed, "The more we look at it, the more we are convinced that you cannot successfully integrate a new product operation such as cable entirely into
the operations of the newspaper."[21]

This theme, and the structure of the three models, repeat themselves as
newspapers have become interested in new media besides cable, especially
videotex and computer information services.

Staff

Regardless of which model has been chosen, cable development has depended on a small group of new media pioneers, working under the aegis of the parent corporation. Many of these staffers have had experience in a variety of media, leading one newsletter to call them "media hybrids." Patricia P. Renfroe, ANPA's director of telecommunications affairs, studied these staffers and found that

> attitude is clearly an important factor: An interest in new technologies and a sense of excitement and adventure are often cited as critical traits of prospective electronic publishing employees. This attitude will also lead employees to innovate, to suggest new approaches and to develop new concepts—which may ultimately make the difference between success or failure.[22]

"Select people who are highly motivated," said Sharon Abbott, coordinator of telecommunications at the *Worcester* (MA) *Telegram and Gazette.* "Select people who are highly motivated, self-confident, who can cope with feelings of isolation as they work alone."[23]

The media hybrids are individualists who must work with the group—a hard type to come by. A Swedish think tank, the Foresight Group, calls such people "intrapreneurs," because they work inside established corporations. As John Naisbitt wrote in *Megatrends:* "The main idea is to reverse the creative inertia in many large corporations by developing the inside entrepreneur."[24]

Newspapers, with the help of the intrapreneurs, have been positioning themselves to respond to even greater changes than cable. Newspapers have wanted to leave behind the rumors of obsolescence and bring forth a new kind of journalist, more effective and more powerful than before. In other words, newspapers are no longer satisfied to react to changes and to be on the defensive.

Taking the Offensive

To take the technological offensive newspapers must follow four basic steps:

> 1. *Recognition of Change*—Newspaper people must become more adept at recognizing change before it is upon them. And when change comes, they must neither overreact nor underreact. Ways of dealing with change must become institutionalized.

2. *Upgrade Operations*—Development must occur fro0 the inside out. Newspapers must continue efforts to modernize plant and personnel. This will enable them to compete better against all comers, print and electronic, established media and new.

3. *The Retooling of the American Journalist*—Although the movement toward precision journalism, spurred by the work of Phillip Meyer and others, is a step in the right direction, journalists must learn to use the new information tools that are being developed. The First Amendment will mean nothing if the journalist is improperly equipped to reach computer-stored information.

4. *Acknowledge the Permanence of Change*—It is time for newspaper managers to accept that the tradition-bound days of journalism are probably behind us, that the pace of change is accelerating, that newspapers must adapt in order to compete and that the stable environment of the past will probably not return.

These are the lessons of the newspaper-cable marriage. Ironically, many newspapers began their cable efforts believing this was a sufficient response to a changing media environment. As it gradually became clear that cable was but a first step, the obvious need arose for a more sophisticated and systematic approach to the challenges—and the opportunities—of the new media.

NOTES

1. "Newspapers Run into an Advertising Slide," *Business Week* (January 18, 1982): 32.

2. David W. Slowthrower, "Sears Exec Warns Newspapers of Impending Linage Losses," *Editor & Publisher* (February 6, 1982): 16.

3. John Morton, "Closing In, Suburbans Increase Pressure on Metros," *Publishers' Auxiliary* (May 17, 1982): 14.

4. Joseph E. Prendergast, Jr., "Newspapers at Mid-Decade and Beyond— Newsprint," *presstime* (January 1985): 30.

5. Richard M. Neustadt, *The Birth of Electronic Publishing* (White Plains, NY: Knowledge Industry Publications, Inc., 1982), p. 7.

6. "$525 a Ton Newsprint May Hurt Newspapers," *Editor & Publisher* (February 20, 1982): 12. In September 1982, author and economist Jon G. Udell compared the rise in newspaper print cost to general inflation. He

found that between 1970 and 1981, the economy experienced a 112% inflation. The price of pulp, paper and related products rose 153% during that time. Producer prices for all commodities increased about 166%—but the prices of newsprint had risen 179% since 1971. See "Newsprint Cost Climbed Faster than Indices," *presstime* (September 1982): 29. Also see "Soaring Expenses Reduce Profits of Typical Daily," *Editor & Publisher* (July 24, 1982): 11.

7. J. Kendrick Noble, Jr., "Four Expert Views," *presstime* (January 1985): 38.

8. Frank J. Savino and Thurman R. Pierce, Jr., "What's the Better Strategy: Survive or Seek Growth?" *presstime* (July 1981): 41–45.

9. John Morton, "The Growth Factors," *Washington Journalism Review* (May 1984): 18.

10. Milt Rockmore, "View from the Top," *Editor & Publisher* (May 1, 1982): 40.

11. Dennis Holder, "Cablemania," *Washington Journalism Review* (September 1982): 36–39.

12. Katharine Graham, in an address to the New England Newspaper Association (February 18, 1982).

13. "Olive Branch," *Publishers' Auxiliary* (May 17, 1982): 7.

14. Howard J. Trienens, "Restriction on Publishing Urged by ANPA," *Editor & Publisher* (March 20, 1982): 13.

15. Robert Marbut. Also see "Publishers Ask Congress to Apply Brakes on AT&T," *Editor & Publisher* (March 20, 1982): 12.

16. There is a debate about which academic institution first offered instruction in electronic publishing. At about the same time the University of Florida made its announcement, three other schools were involved in the field. William C. Porter, managing director of *The Daily Universe* at Brigham Young University, started a student text channel in June 1981. The other two schools are the University of Texas and the University of Wisconsin at Stevens Point. See "New Information Technologies Begin to Appear at J-schools," *presstime* (July 1982): 38.

17. Arthur W. Arundel, in an address before the Suburban Newspapers of America (SNA) Cable TV Seminar, Airlie, VA (October 21, 1981).

18. Steven Effros, "How to Get into Cable and Channel Leasing in Multiple Franchise Areas," in an address to the Suburban Newspapers of America (SNA) Cable TV Seminar, Airlie, VA (October 21, 1981).

19. Donald F. Wright, "Electronic Publishing: How to Use It and Why," *presstime* (February 1982): 25.

20. Dave Clark, manager of Sunflower Cablevision, in a private conversation with the author (October 1985).

21. Phillip H. Power, "The Newspaper's View of Cable," address at the Suburban Newspapers of America (SNA) Cable TV Seminar, Airlie, VA (October 21, 1981).

22. Patricia F. Renfroe and Kathleen Criner, "How to Hire Staff for Electronic Publishing Ventures," *presstime* (January 1982): 38–39.

23. Ibid.

24. John Naisbitt, *Megatrends* (New York: Warner Books, Inc., 1982), p. 204.

4

Evaluating New Media Ventures

Newspapers got their new media ventures up and running, then promptly grew dissatisfied. The market proved difficult to identify. The technology seemed ever-changeable. And after years of newspapers ignoring developments in telecommunications, their initial efforts failed to boost company revenues instantly.

The result was a period of reassessment that affected newspapers of all sizes.[1] Some newspapers forged ahead with new projects despite the obstacles. For example, in 1985 Gannett Co., which was losing millions of dollars on its satellite-transmitted national newspaper, *USA Today,* launched a computer-based information service, USA Today Update, offering news summaries and breaking stories to information vendors such as CompuServe, The Source and others. And Cox Enterprises Inc., a newspaper and cable system owner, announced a call-in talk show and news program: the *Atlanta Journal-Constitution* Video Edition.

But other newspapers decided to scale back. In November 1984 the *Dallas Morning News* ceased text programming on its local cable channel because of low revenue projections. Early in 1985, The Washington Post Co. hedged its investment in Philadelphia and Chicago sports networks by selling some shares to CBS Inc. and to Rainbow Program Enterprises for about $25 million. And Knight-Ridder Newspapers, Inc., cut the staff of its Viewtron videotex operation. The company also sold its share in eight cellular radio applications after the FCC decided to award licenses based on lottery selection rather than on the merits of the applications.

Several types of problems led to this period of reassessment.[2] When newspapers entered the new media field, they heard a great deal about communications synergy, the idea that development in one area of communications could promote advances and products in another. Thus satellite technology contributed to the rise of national newspapers; cheaper microwave transmitters could facilitate LPTV interconnects; timesharing information networks made small, portable computers more useful for journalists, and so forth. But now newspapers were learning about the downside of synergy: lack of development in one area could retard progress in another. For example, A. H. Belo of Dallas, the newspaper and broadcasting conglomerate, signed up 200 customers to pay $10 a month for the Bison database. It offered local news, news wires, TV listings, airline information and local events. But after a $2 million investment, Bison was suspended. The company concluded that home computer penetration simply was not far enough along to support the database product.

Another obstacle, one encountered by many established media companies, was the problem of audience verification. How could the number of LPTV or DBS or cable viewers be established? With online databases, the computer could keep records of what frames of information were called up, how often and for how long. These records were centralized. But each cable system was its own fiefdom. The number of channels would vary from 12 in one system to 120 in another. With so many channels and systems, the audiences could become divided into wafer-thin segments that often defy measurement, at least for local programmers. And advertisers wanted to know what they were paying for.

Still another problem was that of internal ambivalence among company managers. Many secretly wanted the new media projects to fail. This seemed to be partly the problem with CBS's star-crossed CBS Cable, which lost $30 million before the company called it quits. A vice president for Doyle Dane Bernbach, Inc., W. S. James, remarked, "They spent a lot of money and were unrealistic about it being profitable in its first year. But the primary problem was that there was ambivalence on the part of CBS Inc., about the thing. CBS's primary revenue is from broadcasting, and cable is, in a sense, a threat to CBS."[3]

The problems of internal ambivalence, audience verification and negative synergies gradually forced companies to take another look at their interest in the new media. They were beginning to appreciate the high development costs and the slow payoffs that new forms of media—UHF TV, FM radio, telephone—have traditionally had. Often they realized their initial efforts had been unrealistic and poorly planned. Newspaper analyst Christine D. Urban warned, "We have to *think,* not react."[4]

MISTAKES MADE, LESSONS LEARNED

With perfect 20/20 hindsight, it is now clear newspapers made key mistakes as they began to explore the new media. The mistakes must be recognized, lest they be repeated. Mostly, the errors resulted from an overreliance on past media experience in dealing with new problems. The seven major mistakes were:

1. *Transfer of Editorial Product*—The thinking went: "We already have a successful print information product, so we'll reformat it for another medium."

   The idea, of course, was to save money and to use what had worked before. Occasionally the strategy worked. The Dow Jones News Retrieval, for example, relied heavily on the company's news wire and on information from *Barron's* and *The Wall Street Journal.* Even here, however, the information was re-edited, not merely retyped, to meet the needs of the database user.

   Usually information suited for newspaper publication was not well suited for database publishing or other new media use. And if it had been, it would probably have been cheaper in print anyway.

2. *Transfer of Human Talent*—The thinking went: "The advertising department already does a great job of selling newspaper ads. We'll have them sell videotex ads as well."

   Unfortunately, the existing staff's ability to sell newspaper ads can itself hinder its effectiveness with the new media. They sell space instead of time, and they are accustomed to selling print rather than electronic media. While it is probably true that talented salespeople can sell anything, they may have trouble selling different, competing products at the same time. Working on a commission, they will naturally concentrate on the easiest, quickest sell. This is bound to be the already established medium; new media advertising is likely to suffer in the trade-off.

3. *Underestimating the Competition*—The thinking went: "I'll lease a cable channel and sit on it. That will lock out the competition."

   This was not so much a way of coping with a new communications environment as a way of avoiding that unpleasant reality. It assumed that alternatives such as broadcast teletext, videotex, database publishing, LPTV and other new media forms would remain undeveloped.

4. *Failure to Identify a Market*—Although it is hard to believe today, many publishers used to think: "For just $15,000, we'll program a character generator and make money selling cable TV ads."

   In other words, publishers had assumed there would be a market for their product without devoting much time to considering what aspects of their new system would make it superior to existing media. Historically, audiences and markets for new communications media have proved elusive.

5. *Short-Term Thinking*—The thinking went: "After a couple of quick adjustments, we'll be ready to compete."

Probably 9 out of 10 initial investments in new media businesses were money-losers. Yet, newspaper involvement continued, because managers felt they had to learn about new media to continue to grow and compete. The problem of exponentially increasing information outlets could not be solved with a few snap responses. There was no quick fix, and this realization gradually forced managers to plan for the long term.

6. *Insufficient Investment*—The thinking went: "We can save money because the system is automated. We'll spend more later if we have to."

Publishers had to realize they were undertaking more than a reformatting of existing news. They were researching an entirely new form of communications. This could only be done properly with new personnel and increased overhead. Publishers wanted to tie their newspaper computer into the cable, videotex or database system to transfer information automatically. Almost universally, the cost involved was greater than anticipated.

7. *Overreaction*—Some publishers and analysts concluded: "Newspapers are dying out; they're dinosaurs."

Such thinking certainly could not be supported by the average profitability of public newspaper corporations, among the most consistently successful businesses in the country. Some newspapers overreacted to the problems posed by the new media, forgetting that their basic success depended on their editorial quality. It is a mistake for newspapers to divert resources away from their basic business drastically.

A REALISTIC APPROACH TO NEW MEDIA

Having recognized these mistakes, newspaper companies must answer a series of questions about their goals if they hope to develop a more effective, realistic strategy toward the new media. These questions fall into three categories.

The first category consists of identity questions. These include "What do new media have to do with my business?" and "What do we hope to gain by being involved?"

The second category is made up of technological questions: "What are the technological developments most likely to affect our established business?" and "Given changing technology, where can we make a safe investment?"

The third category consists of market questions: "Who will pay how much for what services?" and "How can we test the marketplace?"

Any established communications company must carefully consider each type of question in connection with any new media investment that it might undertake.

Identity Questions

"What business are we in?" is a question continually facing vigilant companies, and nowhere does it come up as frequently as at established media companies.[5] Publishers, editors, writers and account representatives are all uncertain precisely how the new media relate to their work. Much of the confusion stems from the fact that new media information may be displayed on the TV screen. For years, print journalists have resisted what they see as the trivializing effect that television has on news. They have a print chauvinism, the belief that solid reporting occurs only in print. The idea that the new media are television-dependent disturbs them, for these print purists want as little to do with the broadcast media as possible.[6]

Yet this chauvinism overlooks newspapers' proud tradition of developing other media; many radio and television stations were created by newspapers. While print journalists can distance themselves from broadcasters, they cannot undo the historical relationship between print and developing media. If newspaper managers in a print-oriented age considered television and radio relevant to the news business, why should they consider computer databases and videotex less so?

Perhaps it would help to delineate the substantial differences between new media and broadcast TV:

- *Expanded Versus Limited Supply*—The new media offer many outlets—cable, videotex, database publishing, multichannel microwave and others. This means that detailed information can be provided, resulting in greater depth of news coverage, interaction between news organizations and their customers, and the advent of community television.

- *Revenue*—New media generally earn revenue the way newspapers do, through local advertising and subscriptions, plus national ads. This revenue base means the new media must be more responsive to the community.

- *Programming Cost*—Author Ralph Lee Smith believes that cable programming is cheaper to produce and therefore will diversify the use of television.[7] It is possible other new media will become more accessible to the average person than, say, a $200,000 network advertising spot.

- *Heightened Competition*—A gradual erosion of the networks' ratings dominance, because of cable and videocassette recorders (VCRs), means more competition for the advertising dollar. This will gradually force improvements in program quality, although probably not to the radical degree some critics hoped a decade ago.

- *Interactive Uses*—The two-way capabilities of the new media, by which the user can send messages as well as receive them, offer immense marketing possibilities. Shopping at home, banking at home, bill paying at home and other uses are of great interest to retailers and banks. Although videotex trials in London, Miami and elsewhere have been not been too successful, the entrance of IBM and AT&T into the videotex field is a sign that more rapid development of the business may occur.

Given these differences, the new media ought not be confused with network television. But of course the question remains, What do they have to do with printing? It is interesting to note that this same question could be asked of operations that are already firmly ensconced in newspaper plants. What, for example, do computer timesharing or computer mail lists have to do with newspaper publishing per se? How does a total market coverage publication or a job press contribute to newspaper publication?

The justification, of course, is that these are additional revenue sources, that they contribute to the company's overall strategic position and that they seem to fall into the company's definition of its mission. These are the same reasons for newspaper involvement in the new media, and newspapers must accept this broader identity if they are to take advantage of the new communications marketplace. Thus the new media force journalists to think of their jobs in a broader, more ambitious way—as related to all means of communication.

Technology

Given this new sense of identity, managers must also take into account rapidly changing technology. There are two areas to consider: how new technology may threaten the existing newspaper business and how it may affect the new media venture, once the company has decided to follow that route. But understanding these matters depends on predicting the course of technology, an undertaking as puzzling as it is crucial. Anticipating the threat of new technology is a matter of judgment. But it is important to make the most informed judgment possible. Factors such as overhead costs, the cost of developing a new technology and the areas of technology advancing most rapidly must be considered. A communications consultant or an in-house research team is needed to make these kinds of projections.

Because of this uncertainty about technology, business people have made substantial investments with only a feigned confidence about them. They turn to technological desideratum to support their judgment, but uncertainty remains. Thomas A. Crowley, executive vice president of the consulting firm Communications Technology Management Inc., told newspaper people: "The last few years, a lot of money has been poured down rat holes, in an effort to get a hold on all of this. . . . Whether people admit it or not, a lot of that money has been wasted."[8]

Gaining technological expertise is a long-term and open-ended goal. Experts who have spent a great deal of time studying the technologies of communication recognize that there is no clear-cut point at which one can confidently bring a new communications concept to market. Many managers complain that they get increasingly complex problems out of the lab, not solutions.

Of course, technology and the study of technology have a role to play. Managers should do their best to anticipate how change will affect their businesses. But they must do so knowing that technology does not a market make.

Market

Newspapers' increasing new media sophistication is signaled by their shift away from technology and toward the marketplace. They are interested in technology as it might affect their ability to sell products and news. Now they are looking at information systems from the user's rather than from the engineer's point of view.

This leads to an important market question: how will customers respond to manipulating relatively complex information-entertainment devices such as the home computer? Often-told horror stories relate that most TV repair calls involve sets that are out of tuning adjustment or are unconnected to a power source. Will consumers learn how to perform a keyword search on a videotex system?

It is probably true that some will be unwilling or unable to use these systems. But consumers have shown the ability to adapt when it is in their economic interest to do so: examples include self-service gas stations, automatic teller machines, generic-brand shopping and direct-dial telephone calling in place of operator-assisted calls. Nor is limited usage a problem for new media alone. According to the ANPA Foundation, an estimated 23 million Americans are functionally illiterate, and therefore unable to "access" their local newspaper.[9]

Then there is another market question: who will sell the new media? There are two views of the newspaper's role in the new communications environment: the local franchise and the independent entrepreneur.

The Local Franchise

The local franchise holds that newspapers and other local media businesses will fulfill certain programming slots on what are otherwise nationally programmed systems. A teletext system with local windows for community information, to be programmed by the local newspaper, would be one example. Local availabilities on satellite news channels is another. By this scenario, the new media are too expensive for any practical ownership or development on the local level. Large corporations develop the systems nationally, then bring them to the localities. But because local information is needed, some room is left for local news and advertising.

Many newspaper publishers, however, are uneasy about being a local franchise for the new media. They fear this could mean sacrificing the quality control and editorial decisions that make the newspaper credible in the community. The *Louisville Courier-Journal* and the *Louisville Times* is one company concerned about this prospect. According to Robert L. Anderson, cable news service editor and director for the company, "You are already seeing the phenomenon of the communications conglomerates getting into the local market and relegating newspapers to a role as a branch on a tree that has its roots elsewhere."[10]

That is why the company has explored French Antiope-style graphics, a graphics format similar to Telidon, via teletext. The company is also investing in a public-access videotex system. It planned to have 50 videotex terminals in place by the summer of 1985 in public places like malls, hotels and tourist centers.

The Independent Entrepreneur

The course being followed by the *Courier-Journal* is the second view of the newspaper's role in developing the new media: the independent entrepreneur. "Independent" simply means the paper is left free to experiment with the new media in its own community. The independent entrepreneur is determined to maintain its local information dominance, despite the potentially high cost of doing so. A newspaper operating on this model often refuses to help another company gain experience in the local market, and in any case insists on retaining complete editorial control.

Which scenario wins out—the local franchise or the the independent entrepreneur—will largely depend on how much the community will pay for local information provided in some new form. Probably the outcome will vary from market to market. The cost of developing the new media can overwhelm a small company. But a large measure of local responsiveness is often desirable.

Testing the System

Measuring this local responsiveness brings up a third important market question: how will new communications systems be tested in the marketplace? Whether allied with a large company or going it alone, newspapers must have a means of determining which selling methods will work. The obvious answer is to test the product on the market. Methods include questioning people on the services they would like to have; giving people a free sample of the product and seeing how they respond; conducting market research, with elaborate experiments, studies and product trials.

But the untested nature of the new media complicates such research. Most consumers have little knowledge of them or how they work. Explaining the systems takes time and money and may bias the results. It is difficult to demonstrate the value of something that, from the consumer's point of view, does not yet exist.

One way around this is "concept research." Surveyors explain what the new media will do for the consumers. These surveyors then ask the consumers if they like the idea and how they might use the service. But some professionals question the usefulness of whatever information is obtained. "I think that's worthless," says Phillip Meyer, professor at the University of North Carolina's School of Journalism. "It's like asking somebody if he'd want a hula hoop when he's never seen one." Meyer says that newspapers should accept the experimental nature of the new media, spend the money that is needed and take the risks. "That's what entrepreneurs are for," he says.[11]

But many companies, including Knight-Ridder, Time Inc., Gannett and others have tried the experimental route, and they know all too well the cost of randomly exploring the frontier. One certainty is that new media have proven a good way to spend money fast. If spending large sums with an uncertain payback is the only way newspapers can remain independent entrepreneurs, many newspapers will opt out.

APPROACHING THE MARKET

Newspaper analyst Christine D. Urban urges newspapers to undertake a thoughtful approach instead of experimentation. She begins by listing the four universal reasons people consume information:

1. *Surveillance*—To find out what is going on that might affect them.

2. *Social Contact*—To have something intelligent to say at the cocktail party and to be a better informed human being.

3. *Decision Making*—To decide which product to buy, which movie to see, which candidate to vote for or to evaluate the meaning of events—information can be a tool directed to an end.

4. *Simple Pleasure*—Consuming information is a form of entertainment. "I think we often forget that people enjoy reading and they enjoy watching TV," she says. "There is a curiosity and a drive to consume information that has nothing to do with function, only desire."[12]

Some media are suited to surveillance; some may provide more pleasure. Some media deliver information more quickly. Others provide information in detail. By fitting information content with the medium best suited to deliver that particular information, a proper "information fit" is achieved. People are most likely to find it in their interest to use a particular medium when this occurs.

This supposes that when managers are planning a new information product they should meticulously consider what characteristics the information may have and how it can best be formatted for transmission over whatever system is being proposed. This will help develop the best possible match between medium and message. For example, we know that databases have the ability to convey what Urban calls "instantly updatable agate," highly detailed information that changes rapidly. They are particularly useful for stock quotations and travel schedules, which has led some to believe that newspaper classifieds, more than any other current form of advertising, are well suited to the computer medium—a fact of great concern to newspapers.

It is important for managers to proceed with utmost caution through the confusing morass of the new media, yet proceed they must. Long-range thinking becomes important and a manager must learn as much as possible and exercise methodical planning and patience. But this should not be confused with a passive stance. Even Urban concedes that eventually projects have to succeed or fail in the marketplace. The point is that careful planning, not fearful reaction, boosts the chances of success.

CHANGES AND BENEFITS

Market, technology and identity questions have confronted established media companies, and those questions are gradually being answered. Consequently, established media managers are viewing the new media more analytically and more realistically. They carefully analyze the benefits that each medium can provide, and are more conscious of media relativity—the need to combine medium and message to provide an effective communications system, a seamless information benefit to the viewer (and advertiser). The challenge for newspaper companies is to develop information products and services that complement technical delivery systems, to maximize the information's usefulness to the consumer.

These ideas could cause a change in newspapers: traditionally, their heartbeat has been the printing press. It has regulated the tempo, economics and even the language of the business. Production will continue to be important to newspapers throughout this century. But they may also choose a gradual exploration of other delivery systems beside the press.

But the need for a solid editorial product will not change. In a world hungry for accurate information, systems with superior editorial content will continue to thrive. And newspapers are in an excellent position to provide this information content, as long as they remain flexible to new delivery methods. From Urban's point of view,

> Newspapers have one key, unique comparative advantage, and that's the newsroom. Of all the key assets of a newspaper, this is the one that's damn hard for a competitor to replicate.

> It's a protected position, with a tremendous demand base from all the system operators who need information to plug onto this system. As a system operator, newspapers compete with people on an equal basis. It's much more fun, I think, to compete on an unequal basis when you're on the top. And the key issues—the comparative advantage. . . is the information you supply, not the means of delivering it.[13]

In the end, although technology affects how editorial content is delivered, it will not make up for a weak product and should not be the deciding factor for a newspaper planning to invest in the new media. Rather, newspaper managers must answer the relevant market, technology and identity questions and derive a coherent strategy.

STRATEGIES FOR INVESTMENT

Such a strategy will eventually determine the level of investment. No one depth of involvement is right for all companies. The strategy chosen will

depend on the company's goals in the new media, and also on resource availability. But there are four general strategic ways to approach the new media:
the Conceptual Approach, Hold Your Place in Line, Research & Development
Model and Market Experimentation. Once a company has identified its new
media goals, it will match them to one of the following four strategic
courses:

1. *Conceptual Approach*—"Think before you act."
   This strategy is appropriate for companies with limited resources
and those that believe the new media may be a flash in the pan. Such
a company wishes to learn about the new media and to track the
industry trends generally, but plans to undertake little actual investment. After all, the technology is rapidly changing, and the new
media are in flux; an investment now could be wasted if a new
medium makes it obsolete. But by carefully following the new media
business, the company can be ready to move if a solid opportunity
presents itself.
   The strategy offers low cost and flexibility, but a company
pursuing it risks missing opportunities. The competition may seize
an edge, while noninvolvement precludes the staff from getting
hands-on experience that might be valuable later.

2. *Hold Your Place in Line*—"Just in case, let's hedge our bet."
   This is a good strategy for companies with somewhat limited
resources, or for companies that want to buy time through partial involvement before they make a big push later. It gives the newspaper
more assurance that it will not fall behind aggressive competitors
that are directly involved in the new media.
   A company can hold its place in line through buying a character
generator and leasing time on a cable channel. Or a newspaper could
issue a local TV news report for cable or LPTV. The goal is to get
some direct experience, often through a joint venture with a larger
company assuming most of the costs. Holding Your Place in Line
means spending as little as possible until another opportunity comes
along. As a strategy, it costs little and offers the staff some direct
experience. But it is a somewhat defensive maneuver, designed to
keep from losing ground. If the new media are important enough for
the newspaper company to adopt this strategy, then the company's
goals should be reviewed. Holding Your Place in Line is best used as
an interim strategy.

3. *Research & Development Model*—"Communications and our business
   are rapidly changing. Let's prepare."
   This is a good strategy for aggressive companies that want to be in
the forefront of developing new media and that have the resources

to hire the technicians or engineers needed to accomplish this. The strategy calls for well-planned investment in the new media, combined with a research effort to develop new ideas and products. Newspapers that undertake even limited R&D are moving boldly and taking risks to avoid a defensive posture.

4. *Market Experimentation* – "An all-out effort."
  This strategy will appeal to major communications companies that seek to develop, test and introduce their own new media information systems to the public. This involves ownership of information delivery systems such as cable franchises, R&D, market and consumer research, marketing and much more. The move by Gannett into a national newspaper combined with an online database is an example of this sort of major new media undertaking. It assumes the parent company has the mountains of capital needed to develop new communications services. The strategy offers opportunities for market dominance, but its high cost is prohibitive, except for very large corporations. A company pursuing this strategy may suffer from the inefficiencies of experimentation in a changing, primordial market.

These four basic strategies are the ones newspapers should match with their new media goals to determine what to invest in, and how. The strategies will help avoid bad investment of time and money, and eventually they will help earn profits, as described in the following chapter.

NOTES

1. See, for example, Jeff Munsinger, "Publisher Changes Channels on Cable Plans," Virginia Press Association Management File, as quoted from *Missouri Press News* (October 1981): 1.

2. Margaret Genovese, "Cable Television Market Is Still Hot, but Some Papers Get Cold Shoulder," *presstime* (April 1982): 20. Also, "A Cablenews Epitaph: It Was Great While It Lasted," *Electronic Publisher* (October 20, 1981): 4–5.

3. Merrill Brown, "CBS Shows How to Fail With Cable," *Washington Post* (September 16, 1982).

4. Christine D. Urban, "Social Impact of Emerging Technologies," in an address before the American Press Institute's "Newspapers, Telecommunications and Cable TV Seminar," Reston, VA (September 17, 1982).

5. Benjamin B. Tregoe and John W. Zimmerman, *Top Management Strategy* (NY: Simon & Schuster, 1980), pp. 15–38.

6. Sharon Abbott of the *Worcester Telegram and Gazette* said, "When I started working in cable, people in the newsroom were very suspicious. Why was I getting into this?" From "Newspapers and Cable TV," in an address before the American Press Institute's "Newspapers, Telecommunications and Cable TV Seminar," Reston, VA (September 1982).

7. Ralph Lee Smith, *The Wired Nation* (New York: Harper & Row Publishers, 1972), p. 8.

8. Thomas A. Crowley, "Newspaper Strategies in the Developing Marketplace," in an address before the American Press Institute's "Newspapers, Telecommunications and Cable TV Seminar," Reston, VA (September 1982).

9. A study funded by the Ford Foundation put the figure closer to 50 million. See "Chairman's Corner," *presstime* (September 1982): 2.

10. Robert L. Anderson, "Newspapers and Cable TV," in an address before the American Press Institute's "Newspapers, Telecommunications and Cable TV Seminar," Reston, VA (September 1982).

11. David Rambo, "New Services Stir Variety of Questions on Marketing," *presstime* (October 1981).

12. Ibid.

13. Ibid.

5

Profitability and Advertising

The new media are having a historic impact on the way newspaper people think about their business. Newspapers have shifted attention away from cutting costs in existing operations and are considering how to offer entirely new information products as additional revenue sources.

But obstacles to profitability have led critics to question whether newspapers can really profit from the new media. The critics point to the demise of CBS Cable, the Entertainment Channel and some newspaper cable-leased channel efforts as evidence that there often is more talk than income in the new media.

But there is another side to the question that has to do with advertising.

NEW MEDIA ADVERTISING

Most newspapers want to use the new media to sell advertising. Currently there is little advertising on cable compared to the networks, however, and cable is the most developed of the new media. In 1986, cable advertising will produce only a small fraction of revenue compared to basic and premium subscriptions.

Traditionally cable has made money from entertainment, not advertising or information. According to Bill Strange, vice president of cable operator Sammons Communications, "Historically, we're lousy local programmers. We're sellers of entertainment. Historically, we've [collected] so little advertising revenue, we could not even measure it as a percentile of our revenue dollar."[1]

The cable operators have overlooked advertising because they have been too busy building cable systems, they are unfamiliar with the local ad markets and they have viewed local production as a money-losing proposition.

But this is changing. One CATV equipment supplier boasts: "The CATV industry is just now discovering the self-supporting nature of cable advertising and the momentum it can produce."[2] Paul Kagan & Associates, the cable industry analyst, has projected a dramatic rise in cable advertising. Kagan predicts that revenue for the national network satellite channels, including the likes of CNN, ESPN, Black Entertainment Television (BET), USA Network and others, will rise from $606 million in 1985 to $800 million in 1986. By 1990, he projects, cable network ad revenues will be about $2 billion, and national and local spot advertising, most of which is placed with local cable systems, will also show healthy revenue growth. Revenue is projected to increase from $129 million in 1985 to $193 million in 1986, and to approach $633 million by 1990, according to the Cabletelevision Advertising Bureau.[3]

Interest in cable advertising is strong. According to *Advertising Age* magazine, the top 10 users of cable advertising have increased cable expenditures by almost a fourth since 1984.[4] Retailers and manufacturers are particularly interested in the creative potential of cable marketing—the longer "infomercial" formats that attempt a more sophisticated, information-oriented appeal. "From a nervous start, cable advertising is becoming a big business," says *TVC* magazine associate editor Chuck Moozakis.[5]

A major drawback of cable advertising and new media advertising generally is lack of audience verification. Viewers can be so divided among many channels, it can be difficult to count the audience. But despite this uncertainty, local programmers have employed special tactics to sell local advertising:

- *Special Presentation Techniques*—An educational approach may be needed to sell advertising clients unfamiliar with new media. This may include a videotaped proposal.

- *Tag Lines*—Anything to raise the medium's profile will help. One method involves asking viewers to say where they saw the advertisement for a particular product, in return for a discount or other incentive. This gives feedback to the retailer regarding the ad's effectiveness.

- *Contests*—Cable channels must promote their advertising capabilities the same way local TV and radio stations have. This is a weakness of newspapers, which often suffer from a lack of promotional expertise. Accordingly, newspapers introducing new information products must learn to compete for the viewer's time, possibly by having giveaways, games and other promotions.

But despite the rise in expenditures on cable advertising, newspapers have had a difficult time making new media ventures profitable. This is partly because most cable ad revenue goes to national, not local, programmers, and partly because of the high overhead of television programming. The long payoff time in any investment in a new medium is another reason. Given these problems, many newspaper managers wonder aloud if the company's money could be better spent elsewhere.

Newspapers should focus on three avenues toward profit that look promising: the New Media Bureau, Local Availability and the Cable Interconnect.

The New Media Bureau

A text channel can succeed on the basis that a venture that costs little cannot make you lose much. Newspaper technology can funnel classifieds into the cable system automatically, with the utmost efficiency.

An example is Monroe Cable News in Monroe, North Carolina. The text channel there is safely tucked under the wing of the *Enquirer Journal,* a family-owned newspaper with a circulation of 12,000. The text channel depends on two Texscan MSI character generators that program channels 7 and 11 on the cable system. It uses the following equipment:

- Two microcomputer memory controllers (one located at the cable head end a half mile away, the other at the newspaper).

- One TV monitor.

- Two modems to send data from the newspaper to the cable head end.

- One dual floppy disk memory system.

- Two audio receivers at the head end.

- One weather board for updated temperature.

The cost of this equipment as of this writing would be about $50,000. There are also monthly operating costs:

- A contractual lease agreement based on a percentage of gross revenues (no flat monthly rate).

- Equipment amortization on a seven-year straight line.

- Subscription to AP news service: $49.50 per week.

- Leased telephone line to head end, $12 per month.

- Ten percent of gross for advertising sales commission.

The cable news director, Mark F. Ashcraft, says the newspaper sells 20-second spots that appear at least once an hour throughout the day for $108.[6] Classified ads are handled through the newspaper's classified department.

Initially Ashcraft was the only staffer. He told the South Carolina Press Association that a month after advertising start-up, Monroe Cable was breaking even because of its low overhead. While the revenue is minuscule now, it demonstrates that new media are not automatically money-losers for newspapers. Similarly, Missouri's *Excelsior Springs Daily Standard* achieved a break-even point within four months of start-up, according to *Electronic Publisher,* an industry newsletter.[7] Such examples show that cable text, on a bare-bones basis, can sometimes be self-supporting.

A word of warning, however: cable text does not risk much, and it does not stand to gain much, either. Cable text is not a sexy product. Systems that break even on the books may run in the red when management time and effort are calculated. And in any case, they are only sufficient for those companies that have adopted the defensive Hold Your Place in Line strategy discussed in the previous chapter.

Local Availability

The rationale for inserting ads locally via national satellite channels such as MTV, CNN and others is that programming itself is too expensive to produce. Local availabilities—one- or two-minute windows offered periodically to local programmers as an incentive—mean the newspaper can concentrate on producing advertising.

The ANPA has observed a "very definite trend" toward newspaper video production. A 1982 survey of 54 newspapers involved in telecommunications showed 21 programming the local inserts on cable satellite channels, including *The Des Moines Register & Tribune* and the *Bangor (ME) Daily News.*[8]

Gannett's *Fort Myers News-Press* has experimented with local availability advertising, having invested about $100,000 in equipment, including cameras, character generators, videocassette recorders, a console and a portable VCR, monitors, and an editing deck. The Southern Cablevision system has about 25,000 subscribers. Prices for a 30-second spot range from $7 to $20.[9] With four 30-second ads each hour, 24 hours a day, the revenue figures for video inserts begin to look a little more interesting than cable text. But the initial expense and operating cost are greater, too. And the newspaper's audience is still limited by the size of the cable system.

Cable Interconnect

The audience limitations inherent in a single system can be overcome by connecting cable systems so that they can air the same programming. This typically combines higher cost and risk with a higher profit potential.

The interconnect is an increasingly popular way to tie several markets together for advertising purposes. In May 1985, Cable AdNet Central, a group of 10 cable systems serving 150,000 subscribers in Pennsylvania, hired Cable Networks Inc. to sell cable advertising. About 40% of the households in Harrisburg, Lancaster, Lebanon and York are hooked to members of the interconnect. CNI, a partnership of Sammons Communications and several other cable and broadcasting companies, sells advertising on cable systems and interconnects in nearly 90 markets.[10]

An equally ambitious effort is Gill Cable network in California. The idea is to connect each cable head end in the region with a microwave frequency link. Called Cable Antenna Relay System (CARS), it must be approved by the FCC before it can be used. With proper switching equipment, the interconnect allows several cable systems to carry the same local program simultaneously. Success for CARS depends on whether cable operators who battled each other during franchising can learn to cooperate closely.

CARS is expensive. Each microwave link may cost between $50,000 and $100,000. But by restricting programming to local cutaway advertising, production expenses can be minimized. The interconnect should begin with this strict focus, and only later extend into local origination programming (if it can afford to do so).

An important obstacle to newspaper involvement in cable interconnects exists: FCC rules stipulate that a CARS license can only be held by a cable operator or by a nonprofit consortium of cable operators. This means newspapers must obtain a cable partner, or be a cable operator, to have an application approved. But at that point the cable operator is very likely to ask the newspaper, "What do I need you for?"

The laws are frustrating for newspapers that believe the cable interconnect offers one of the most profitable areas for investment. They cannot compete with a company like Centel Inc., for example, which plans to serve 16 different cable systems in Chicago and its suburbs. Its $3 million interconnect system will serve 125,000 households initially and could eventually amass 1.5 million or more viewers. An audience of this size begins to solve some revenue problems.[11]

But Centel and interconnects like it could still work to newspapers' advantage. Centel's Videopath is licensed as a common carrier, which means it will rely on other companies to provide the advertising. Bob Cohen, the president of the Chicago Cable Advertising Network, says he plans to charge $60 to $100 per 30-second spot on Videopath, and that the time may be sold in part by newspapers. *Cable Vision Magazine* reports:

> Cohen is making his pitch for the Videopath to account groups and media buyers, and to broadcast and newspaper media as well. Indeed, a key part of Cohen's Videopath strategy is to sell the inter-

connect ad connection as part of a package that utilizes a balanced mix of various media.[12]

One might ask what newspapers could offer cable operators in an interconnect package, and the answer is advertising sales know-how. Cable operators, whether individual or in consortiums, know little about the local advertising marketplace. They do not want to put further strains on cash flow by hiring advertising personnel. This would seem to leave newspapers in the driver's seat when it comes to selling cable advertising.

Interconnects are potentially profitable. But they are no gold mine. Audience verification is still a problem. Advertisers want to know how many viewers are watching at a given time, and it is uneconomical to determine viewership fragmented into many small groups watching different cable channels.

Ironically, with a hardwire link to the home, cable is potentially the most verifiable medium around. Computer monitoring of channel selection would provide advertisers with a wealth of information. But the technical and privacy problems that would have to be overcome are considerable.

PROFITABILITY, ADVERTISING AND OTHER NEW MEDIA

Of course, cable is not the only new medium with profit potential. The problem is that less developed media, such as videotex, cellular radio and optical disks, require huge investments before they return the first dollar of revenue. This tends to preclude many independent newspapers from participating in the race to make the new media economically profitable. Small newspapers will have to determine their choices carefully and realistically.

In any case, here is where the best profit opportunities lie:

Database Publishing

Some newspapers and newspaper companies have already had success in this medium. The best example is Dow Jones News Retrieval, a business-oriented computer information service that offers data from *Barron's*, *The Wall Street Journal*, newswires and other print-based publications. Dow Jones News Retrieval, as of this writing, has about 200,000 subscribers.

Dow Jones is but one of a score of "information supermarkets" that collect vast stores of information deliverable to the home or business computer via telephone. Some of the other supermarkets include: The Source, owned by *Reader's Digest;* Vu-Text, a newspaper database owned by Knight-Ridder; Nexis, owned by Mead Data Corp.; and Dialog, owned by the Lock-heed Corp. These systems, which often cost tens of millions of dollars to create and market, make money through subscription and usage fees paid by the information consumer.

Another way to profit from database publishing without operating an entire system is to sell information to the information supermarkets. For example, Mead Data Corp. has purchased the rights to the full text of *The New York Times,* which it then stocks on the electronic shelves of its super-market. ABI/Inform, a service owned by the publisher of the *Louisville Courier-Journal Times,* abstracts business publications. As of February 1985, the complete texts of more than 20 newspapers could be read on computer databases.[13] Hundreds of other print publications are also available, including *The Japan Economic Journal, The Toronto Globe and Mail, Encyclopaedia Britannica* Library Files, AP, Reuters and UPI. Although advertising on data-bases (as distinguished from videotex) is rare, the publisher makes money whenever the publication is summoned to the terminal screen of a home or business user.

Videotex (Public Access)

While videotex generally seems restricted to very large corporations, public-access videotex has attracted the attention of somewhat smaller companies. Public-access videotex includes the computer-screen terminals at shopping malls, hotels, airports and other locations. Their bright, colorful graphics are attractive to advertisers.

A subsidiary of the *Courier-Journal* and *Louisville Times* Co. hopes to have some 50 public-access videotex Metroguide terminals installed around the city by 1986, in hotels, in an arts center and elsewhere. A Canadian videotex com-pany, Infomart, has licensed its Teleguide terminals to several American news-paper companies that want to offer public-access videotex, including the *Arizona Republic,* the *Phoenix Gazette* and McClatchy Newspapers. A sub-sidiary of the Tribune Co. of Chicago, Tribune Media Services Inc., has in-stalled terminals in Orlando, Florida, hotels for its Video Guide service.

One public-access project, VideoTimes in Davenport, Iowa, has a usage rate of 20,000 pages a day for its eight terminals. The database includes 1500 pages of information. Project Manager Joan M. Allison said a survey of Video-Times users shows that 43% of them use the service every time they go to their mall to shop. However, it is not yet clear whether the enthusiasm of the users will translate into revenue dollars for the parent company, the *Quad-City Times,* a Lee Enterprises paper.[14]

Multichannel Microwave

In 1983 the FCC proposed a new use of the microwave frequency spectrum: multichannel microwave. The goal is to expand the present microwave capability of one channel (MDS) to several channels offering different types of programming.

Whether multichannel microwave can evolve into a newspaper profit center is open to question. The FCC has decided to regulate multichannel microwave as a common carrier, which means the system owner cannot control programming content (just as the telephone company cannot control the phone messages of its users). For First Amendment reasons, newspapers want to stay well clear of any common-carrier restrictions. But another consideration is what role, if any, local news and information will play in multichannel microwave services.

One company making a major push into multichannel microwave is Microband, an MDS system supplier based in New York. Its service, called Urbanet, is already available on a limited basis in New York City's uncabled regions. Urbanet, scheduled to be marketed in the top 30 uncabled urban areas throughout 1986, will mix satellite basic and pay services with over-the-air broadcast channels. Newspapers will have to work with microwave companies such as Microband to see if they can participate profitably in multichannel microwave.[15]

Cellular Mobile Radio

The FCC began accepting applications for this service in June 1982, and several newspapers have since become involved. The Washington Post Co., for example, filed applications for licenses in Baltimore, Detroit, Miami and Washington, DC. McCaw Communications Companies, 45% owned by Affiliated Publications (the publisher of the *Boston Globe*), has filed for licenses in San Francisco-Oakland, Denver-Boulder, Kansas City, Missouri, and San Jose, California.

A future possibility is that users may one day use mobile radio to access a database while on the road. "It's definitely a possibility . . . that we and a lot of others possibly will be looking to develop," says Linda Urben of Advanced Mobile Phone Services Inc., a Bell System subsidiary.[16]

Ironically, reporters will be among the first to benefit from the expansion of mobile telephone use made possible by the cellular technology. Two West Coast publishers, the *Los Angeles Times* and the *Register* of Orange County, California, have already experimented with cellular mobile radiophones. Using a small portable computer such as a Radio Shack Model 100, combined with radio telephone communications, gives a reporter much more mobility. The reporter no longer has to be near a standard telephone to transmit the story. The *Register* used six leased cellular car phones during its coverage of the Los Angeles Summer Olympics. "You can be almost anywhere and be able to transmit a story," said Gary Lycan, assistant managing editor.[17]

These are all examples of profitable opportunities for newspapers. But newspapers should know that, in their desire to make money marketing the new media to the community, they are not alone. One of the most successful marketers of local cable advertising, for instance, is Palmer Cablevision of Florida, owned by a local radio station in Naples. Television companies are also interested in cable. "In increasing numbers," reports *Cable Marketing* magazine, "telecasters are adopting a join-them-if-you-can't-lick-them policy." An example is WMTV of Madison, Wisconsin, which acquired three channels from the local cable operator. Asked by broadcast colleagues why the company was involved in cable, the station's general manager replied, "If we didn't do it, someone else would."[18]

How much newspapers want to participate in the new media is up to them. But they should formulate their research-and-development strategies with the knowledge that new media systems can also be programmed by competitors if the newspaper decides not to step in and experiment. Those newspapers that do get involved should be realistic about their profits. Communications analyst Paul Bortz, recalling the days when many specialized cable channels were expected to flourish along the model of specialty magazines, has noted the radically different economics of those two industries. A magazine's editorial product costs only about 20% to 30% of the total operating cost of the magazine. Production costs of well-produced video, at about $700,000 per hour of on-air network programming, "can easily be 90% of total costs," Bortz says.[19] When one considers that A. C. Nielsen tracks only 6 of the 60 national satellite channels due to audience fragmentation, it becomes clear that obstacles to profitable cable programming will remain formidable.[20] It will be up to those newspapers that do get involved to monitor their progress carefully.

NOTES

1. William B. Strange, Jr., "Economics of the Cable Industry—Advertising and Cable," in an address to the Suburban Newspapers of America (SNA) Cable TV Seminar, Airlie, VA (October 1981).

2. "Cable Advertising," a booklet published by Texscan, MSI company.

3. Statistics from Paul Kagan & Associates, as provided by the Cabletelevision Advertising Bureau.

4. Sallie Rose Hollis, "Channels Answer Interactive Call," *Advertising Age* (May 30, 1985): 26.

5. Chuck Moozakis, "Local Advertisers: Why We Use Cable," *TVC Magazine* (July 15, 1982): 45–47.

6. Mark F. Ashcraft, "Newspaper Cable: Why Should You Be Interested," in an address before the South Carolina Press Association, Greenville, SC (February 1981).

7. "Case Study," *Electronic Publisher* (May 20, 1982): 3–4.

8. Kathleen Criner and Raymond B. Gallagher, "Newspaper-Cable TV Services: Current Activities in Channel Leasing and Other Local Service Ventures," ANPA report (February 1983): 4–5.

9. Andrew Radolf, "Gannett Papers Ready for Cable TV services," *Editor & Publisher* (May 15, 1982): 20.

10. "Ad-Vantage," *Broadcasting Magazine* (May 20, 1985).

11. Victor Livingston, "A Medium of Choice," *CableVision* (August 23, 1982): 20–22.

12. Ibid.

13. In fact, Knight-Ridder's "Vu-Text" has signed service contracts with at least 44 newspapers nationwide. See Bev Smith, "VU/TEXT–Newspaper 'Morgue' Reincarnated as Online Vendor," *Information Today* (October 1984): 15.

14. Elizabeth Donovan, project assistant manager, private conversation with the author (October 5, 1985).

15. "Microwave Offers Alternative," *Advertising Age* (May 30, 1985): 14.

16. Linda Urben, "Cellular Radio To Increase Mobile Phones' Reach," *Publishers Auxiliary* (April 5, 1982). Also see Andrew Radolf, "Newspapers See Riches in Mobile Phones," *Editor & Publisher* (June 12, 1982): 9.

17. George Garneau, "Reporters Getting To Test Mobile Cellular Phones," *Editor & Publisher* (February 9, 1985): 26.

18. Maurine Christopher, "New Cable Acceptance Shown," *Cable Marketing* (April 1982): 14. Also see Art Siemering, "A Marriage of Convenience," *Advertising Age* (April 5, 1982) and "Threat to Radio from Cable TV Cited by Agency," *CableAge* (July 12, 1982): 40.

19. Kathleen Criner and Jane Wilson, "New-technology Players Jockey for Position," *presstime* (November 1984): 23.

20. Ibid. Bortz, a communications analyst of the Denver-based consulting firm Browne, Bortz & Coddington, has also warned the economics of the new media require long-term planning. "You must realize you're getting into a business now, so that you'll be in it by the 1990s," he told publishers. See "Consultant's Caveat: Don't Forget the Basics," *Electronic Publisher* (March 10, 1982): 4.

6

Community Television

The newspaper's relationship with its community was aptly described by veteran newsman Tom Wicker in what he called his First Law of Journalism:

> That so human a creature as a newspaper inevitably reflects the character of its community. And I believe that the American press is neither heroic nor villainous, but that it mirrors rather well the character of the American community.[1]

The country's rich tradition of community journalism should not be taken for granted. Ben Bagdikian writes that, unlike the European and Japanese tradition, in which a few national newspapers serve the entire nation, American news is fixed in the local community, and the typical American consumer receives it from a local private enterprise.

But compare this vision of community newspapers with television news coverage. "Local television" is a TV station broadcasting from up to 20 or 30 miles away, beaming one signal to scores of communities within an area of several hundred square miles. Newspaper coverage operates on an "umbrella model" of readership, whereby an individual may subscribe to one or more metropolitan dailies, a suburban daily and even a community weekly: the subscriber can choose the level of coverage desired. While a local TV viewer may be able to choose among half a dozen stations, the stations are all appealing to the same market area. Inner-city residents, suburbanites and rural residents—groups with vastly different interests—all watch the same network affiliates.

Thus, local TV news has been unable to reflect the character of the communities because it serves one large region. Consider, for example, a broadcasting textbook definition of local news as news of the city in which the television station lies, or within the station's reception range, sometimes to include anything covered by the station's own news staff.[2] Because anything "within the station's reception range" is local, affiliates and independents cannot claim to reflect the individual characters of towns and cities within their region. To the extent that residents make buying and other decisions locally, this is a serious limitation. Veteran newscaster David Brinkley comments:

> . . . a newspaper can print items most of its readers don't give a damn about, because those who don't give a damn about it can skip it, and go on to something else. We can't.

> So what does that mean? In my opinion, it means we should not put a story on the air unless we honestly believe it's interesting to at least 10% of the audience. Preferably more. But at least 10%.[3]

This effectively means coverage by the affiliates on a community level is rare, and routine coverage on the network level is virtually impossible. As one NBC news producer said facetiously, local news for networks is "news occurring outside of Washington or New York."[4]

New media are a tremendous opportunity to change this imbalance and to make television far more versatile than before. The extent to which community television will evolve remains to be seen. But technically, with LPTV, multichannel microwave and cable, the potential exists for every community to have its own local news program.

COMMUNITY TELEVISION—A DEFINITION

Community television is targeted more precisely than network television to a specific audience, region or viewer interest. It is more like community newspapers than network affiliates in this regard. Because of the audience limitation, it may directly depend on the host community for support and survival. In short, we can define community television as video programming that covers the interests of a specific locality. The programs are often produced by members of that community.

Community television may have an important impact on society. For the first time, local politicians might have a "TV image," similar to those of regional and national news figures. Viewers might sit at home and watch live town and city council proceedings: youth club games might be televised; a citizen might appear beneath studio lights to make a pitch for whatever pet cause. In other words, the Brinkley 10% Rule need no longer apply.

Development of Community Television

For decades, universities have supported local television programming to serve their communities of teachers and students. Likewise, major corporations such as Xerox, Mobil and Arthur Young have been using television to train and inform their corporate communities for years. But the precise roots of community television are obscure and seem to be entwined with the advent of new media in general and cable television specifically.

In fact, the political nature of the cable franchising process gave community television its biggest boost. During the heated cable battles of the 1970s, communities expressed interest in local TV coverage, and cable companies offered them production facilities in hopes of wooing politicians to their cause. Some companies merely allocated a cable channel for local programming. Some invested $50,000 to $100,000 in cameras and other equipment, but without hiring staffers trained to use them. With community members intimidated by the hardware, and without anyone to explain it, much of this equipment was placed in a corner and forgotten. But for major franchises, hundreds of thousands of dollars were spent on staff and studio equipment.

In fairness to the cable operators, they often felt that a buyers' market for cable had forced them to make imprudent promises to get the franchise. Spending valuable staff time on community television was not a shrewd way for the average system manager to advance. This often left them in the paradoxical situation of hoping their substantial investment in production equipment would go unnoticed by potential users in the community.

Since then, however, communities have developed defenses that make it more likely the equipment will be used. Now during franchising, or when a franchise comes up for renewal, they may ask for a list of full-time staffers responsible for local production. They may require cable operators to list total community television programming hours to be aired each week.

On the other hand, a concerned community must play more than a watchdog role if it wants viable programming. It is in the interests of community groups, schools or newspapers to provide the programming to relieve the cable operator of as much expense as possible. Otherwise the cost is eventually reflected in higher rates. The cable industry has considered CATV public access a money-loser for years, and although this refractory attitude may perplex newspapers, someone has to assume the responsibility for programming—possibly the residents of the community.

Leased-Channel Negotiations

No set guidelines for negotiating cable TV leases exist. An average lease runs two to five years, sometimes with options to renew. But leases have been

negotiated that run for one year or for the entire length of a 20-year franchise. Newspapers generally seek to reserve one channel on the system, either
for text or video news. A few newspapers have leased several channels on one
system—one channel for text news and one for video. The two-minute "local
cutaway" windows available on some national cable channels (and reserved
for local advertising) have also caught the eye of newspaper programmers,
with leases negotiated for these as well. The newspaper's goal is to obtain as
much airtime as it might need, but to preserve complete editorial control over
how it is used.

Compensation to the cable operator also varies considerably from lease to
lease. Some payment formulas are: a percentage of profits to the operator, a
flat payment each month (a rental), a set fee per subscriber per month or
some form of trade, such as newspaper advertising for cable channel usage.

Typically, a cable operator may determine a channel's value by dividing
the total number of channels in the system into the total cost of building it,
thereby assigning each channel an equal fraction of the total cost. But a newspaper seeks *viewers,* not a channel for its own sake. A balance must be struck
between the cable operator's need for improved cash flow and the newspaper's
desire to experiment affordably. And the operator's local programming
commitments—which the newspaper will be fulfilling—should be considered,
too. In Arlington, VA, a cable company paid more than $250,000 to a
community group in return for community TV production.

COMMUNITY TELEVISION AND LPTV

Although newspaper interest in cable-leased channels has cooled, some
newspapers are looking to low-power television to access the airwaves without the problems of leasing. Newspapers have filed more LPTV applications
with the FCC than any other media group. By 1985 the ANPA estimated that
of the more than 35,000 applications filed, 5,000 were from newspapers.
The newspapers involved included: Gannett Community Television Inc.;
Sowers Newspapers Inc., publisher of the *Rolla (MO) Daily News;* and Bell
Press Inc., publisher of weekly newspapers in Ladysmith and Barron County,
Wisconsin.

A major question mark is the economics of LPTV, given the costs of con-
structing the stations, estimated at $350,000 by *Channels* magazine. John
Boler, of Bemidji, Minnesota, spent an estimated $600,000 getting the first
LPTV station on the air in 1981. In Chicago, veteran broadcaster Charles
Woods spent $750,000 just to buy out opponents contending for the
license.[5]

An ANPA publication observes:

> Few new technologies have been profitable at first. Radio (first AM and then FM), television (VHF and then UHF), cable and pay TV were not initially profitable. Some—as with FM radio and UHF television—took years to overcome limitations and exploit their strengths. Low-power TV may be the same.[6]

Despite the costs of construction and the governmental licensing process, which tends to move at a glacial pace, newspapers remain interested in LPTV as a method of providing community television, for several reasons:

- To avoid lease agreements; to be the owner.

- To serve minorities that have traditionally been under-represented by established media—the reason then-FCC chairman Charles Ferris proposed the service in the first place.

- To operate a station that might later join a network of LPTV stations.

- To gain further experience in the new media.

MULTICHANNEL MICROWAVE

Another potential path for community television is multichannel microwave TV, also known as wireless cable. Three such operations are planned for 1985. They are Movie Systems Inc., in the Milwaukee area, a six-channel system; Pay TV of Greater New York, a five-channel service targeting the outer boroughs of that city; and Premier Communications Networks Inc., a six-channel service in the San Francisco-San Jose area. The extent of local programming remains to be determined. One four-channel service in the nation's capital, American Family Inc., offers, among other things, a regional sports service, Home Team Sports.

With users expected to pay monthly fees of between $25 and $35 for the multichannel microwave service, its viability as a medium for community television may depend on subsidization from pay-TV revenues. (For further discussion of multichannel microwave, see Chapter 2.)

COMMUNITY TELEVISION PROGRAMMING

At the first LPTV convention, held in Washington, DC, newspaper publisher Orville Rickerson explained why he and many other newspaper people are interested in community television:

The small towns across this country still have not had their city councils and their school boards covered live. Many of us in this room have covered school board meetings as a newspaper journalist, and we can appreciate the healthy impact on a community of the live TV coverage of such meetings.[7]

It was a noble concept. If big-city meetings were important enough for TV coverage, why not town meetings as well? After all, which viewers were more likely to be directly affected by such proceedings: those in a large metropolis or those in a small town?

But whether the signal is transmitted by cable, LPTV or multichannel microwave, any decision on what to cover locally must also hinge on costs. First, there is the cost of equipment—a $250,000 for a stripped-down studio package would not be unusual. Then there is the expense of technical staff to consider: producer, director, camera operator, sound technician, studio technician, talent and so forth—in addition to the technical staff required to operate the transmission equipment and install signal decoders.

A single network TV camera may cost twice the annual operating budget of a community television station. So the question arises: what programming can be done well on an economy basis? Nightly TV news programs will rarely be up to standard TV quality. Independently staged productions are often more appealing, which no doubt accounts for the plethora of exercise and dance classes, music concerts and sporting events that are so popular on many cable TV channels.

Newspapers involved in local origination realize what an expensive and dubious proposition local programming can be. When a newspaper identifies itself with a community television program, it wants that program to be top-notch—not a laughingstock. But top-notch talent is expensive; top-notch equipment, exorbitant. Viewers have to be educated to accept community television for what it is . . . a reflection of the community itself. It is not slick news teams, sitcoms or elaborate talk shows.

On a shoestring budget, it is up to the community to make the project work. While networks speak of holding a mirror up to society, the community must hold a mirror up to itself. In the search to operate economically, other local production facilities should not be overlooked. These may include corporate, educational or even hobbyist programmers. Many libraries and schools have video production equipment. A $250 investment in a used VHS or Betamax half-inch recorder enables video to be transferred from one mode to another. Often students can be commissioned as volunteers. An article in the *National High School Broadcasters Newsletter* remarked: "Although news production is a specialization, its nature as a synthesizer of the world/community seems to facilitate satisfying most, if not all, needs for a liberal education in TV production."[8]

Other tips to the would-be programmer:

- Expect audience fragmentation to be severe because of multiple channels. The advertising rate card should be structured to allow a buildup of impressions over a long period—at least a month.

- Promotion is critical to the success of community TV. Unless viewers learn to tune in at the right time, they may miss the show they want to see. Posters, bumper stickers, games on the air and advertisements on the local radio station are all-important devices to raise viewer awareness.

- The best time seems to be just before or just after the network news shows. Try to avoid competing with the affiliates.

In short, community television programmers should set modest, reasonable goals and realize that competition for viewer attention is stiff.

THE NEWSPAPER'S ROLE

Newspapers can help. Viewers, perplexed by the increasing array of channels and programs, repeatedly ask the newspaper to provide them with a special TV section or tab. It should be profitable for the newspaper to provide this.

And of course the newspaper should exploit its own resources which, surprisingly, are so close to home they are often overlooked or underemployed. The advantages the newspaper brings to any local programming effort begin with the valuable asset of community goodwill. Newspapers are established voices in their communities. Although they are trusted only to varying degrees, the residents must believe them to be useful, or they would go out of business. Just using the newspaper's logo can be an asset for a community programmer who seeks to establish credibility and, depending on the quality of the program, may be good publicity for the newspaper besides.

Other assets of the newspaper are more concrete. These include the newspaper's information-gathering expertise. In rural communities, the newspaper is often a natural clearinghouse for information of all types, information often relevant to broadcasting, including that old standby, live coverage of election results.

The newspaper is also a clearinghouse for talent. What newspaper reporters may lack in polish they make up for in expertise. They are especially useful in providing insight and commentary. And columnists, often expert in movies, sports and other entertainment fields that lend themselves to TV, may choose to develop their own video features. Reporters may cover news events strictly for the newspaper or also for community TV. But if their specific reports cannot be used for some reason—newspaper managers may complain about "scooping themselves"—there is no reason their talents cannot be used, if they want to experiment with TV.

Many experts at the newspaper—reporters, graphic artists, community correspondents—can bolster any community TV effort. But there is a note of caution. Perhaps in response to the enforced passivity of broadcast TV, viewers have become very particular about what they expect to see on television. A flashy tie, an eccentricity of speech, a bead of sweat or slight nervousness—any of these details can provoke viewer criticism.

How significant community television becomes, therefore, is ultimately up to those who use and view it. It is hoped that community television will mean a better informed public, one less impressed or influenced by television production techniques, whether in advertising or as part of political campaigns. But this depends: community television is no stronger than the community it serves. After all, community members will be operating the cameras, performing as talent and in one way or another absorbing the costs. As Wicker said of newspapers, community TV will come to mirror rather well the character of the community.

NOTES

1. Tom Wicker, *On Press* (New York: Viking Press, 1978), p. 19.

2. Irving E. Fang, *Television News, Radio News* (Champlin, MN: Rada Press, 1980), p. 386.

3. Ibid., p. 187.

4. Edward Jay Epstein, *News From Nowhere* (New York: Random House, 1973), pp. 190–91.

5. Charles Woods, "Newspapers Among Early Winners as FCC Opens Low-power TV Sweepstakes," *presstime* (April 1982): 25.

6. "Low Power Television Marketing Considerations," (An ANPA information packet prepared by the ANPA Department of Telecommunications Affairs): 9.

7. Orville Rickerson, as quoted during the first LPTV Conference, Washington, DC (February 1982).

8. Bill Doerken, "Vo-Tech Center Produced Cable TV News," *National High School Broadcasters Newsletter* (vol. V, no. 2, August 1982): 1–3.

7

Videotex

Videotex is the international branch of the communications revolution, just as community television is the grass roots branch. Multinational companies, often subsidized by their governments, are competing fiercely to develop videotex, a new communications service. Different types of videotex are being offered by the French (Antiope), the British (Prestel), Canada (Telidon) and several companies in the United States. The competition and the unpredictable market mean that, in the uncertain world of communications, videotex is the least certain element of all.

WHAT IS VIDEOTEX?

There are even disagreements about what videotex is. Debate centers on what point a computer-generated text service becomes a videotex service. This is because there are two types of videotex: text only, and text and graphics. The text-only services are the "information supermarkets" discussed earlier: CompuServe, Dow Jones News Retrieval, Vu-Text and others. They currently serve an estimated 400,000 subscribers in the United States. This type of videotex relies on an electronic code to produce letters on the computer terminal, called the American Standard Code for Information Interchange, or ASCII (pronounced "ask-ee").

The other videotex form uses a code called the North American Presentation Level Protocol Syntax, or NAPLPS (pronounced "nap-lips"). NAPLPS is able to draw colorful graphics—but not pictures—on the terminal. Currently, three commercial services use text and graphics: Viewtron, Gateway and KeyCom. As of 1985 they were struggling along with fewer than 5,000 customers among them. Unlike the information supermarkets, none of them was making money.[1]

What has most captured publishers' imagination about videotex is the idea of an unlimited information resource available at the touch of a finger. But this is a two-edged sword; publishers also worry that videotex might someday replace newspapers as the new medium of record. However, they are also interested in video capability: the display of colorful pictures or graphics. Newspaper publishers recognize that much of their advertising revenue comes from ads highly dependent on pictures: real estate, retail and general business. A deep database, meaning one that stores a great deal of information, might combine with video capability to take some advertising away. But if the system were owned by the newspaper, it might earn the company revenue.

The most talked-about threat is to classified advertising. An electronic information system with comprehensive information could offer the subscriber "superclassified ads." The user could instruct the computer to search for all 1978 Buicks on sale with fewer than 150,000 miles on the odometer, blue in color and with dented left fenders. The computer could list all the vehicles meeting this classification and could even display an image of a car. If such services became widely available, publishers wonder, would readers continue wading through newsprint classified copy? And about a third of newspaper advertising revenues are generated from classified ads.

It remains to be seen whether videotex will become a medium of superclassification. Viewtron has experimented with videotex ads and has not made anywhere near enough money to offset its losses. But some interesting experiments are under way. Fisher-Stevens Inc., for example, has started a news bulletin service combined with an electronic version of *Physicians' Desk Reference,* a compendium of pharmaceutical information provided by drug manufacturers. The computer information service, called Phycom, has attracted 17 pharmaceutical companies, each paying up to $750,000 yearly to advertise its wares to doctors. But this goes beyond classified advertising.[2]

HISTORICAL DEVELOPMENT OF VIDEOTEX

Videotex has been operating in some form for more than a decade. Its origins go back to a British attempt to merge the telephone and the computer with television in a service that would use regular telephone lines to link a home terminal or television set with a database. By 1974, a group of engineers fashioned a working model of it, named Prestel. Gradually the model was modified and improved, and by September 1979, Prestel ceased to be an experimental model and became a commercial enterprise.[3]

It is now generally acknowledged that the introduction of Prestel was ill conceived. Unrealistic growth rates were projected for the new system. The subscription level remains at about 10% of expectations. Despite this, Prestel remains the largest text-and-graphics database in the world as measured by pages (or frames) of information, with more than 200,000.[4]

U.S. communications companies were not as involved as the Europeans during the early development of videotex. This resulted in part because their existing communications networks were more efficient, and also because efforts of foreign companies were subsidized by their governments.

THE CURRENT STATUS OF VIDEOTEX

Today the prize market for videotex, both for domestic and foreign firms, is the United States. There are several reasons: the high penetration of television (97 percent of United States homes), the rapid growth of cable links that might be used to transmit data, the steady increase in number of home computers, and the American adaptability to electronic gadgets.

It is interesting to note that two of the three commercial text-and-graphics services in the United States, Viewtron and Gateway, are owned by newspaper companies. The other one, Keyfax, was partly owned by newspaper publisher Field Enterprises, which pulled out of its joint venture with Centel Corp. and Honeywell Inc. when it sold the *Chicago Sun-Times*.

Viewtron is owned by Knight-Ridder and debuted in southern Florida in October 1983. It was the nation's first attempt at a commercially viable videotex system. The information system offers leisure and entertainment information ("Fitness Expert," "Recipe Exchange," "Weekend Getaways") and many services such as home banking, stock quotes and company profiles. Company officials hoped Viewtron would attract 5,000 subscribers in its first year, but the response was only about half that. The company reacted by laying off about 20% of its full-time employees and has sustained losses of over $17 million.[5]

Undaunted by Viewtron's losses, Gateway opened shop in October 1984, serving three affluent counties located south of Los Angeles, California. Gateway's subscriber count is below Viewtron's, but is still more than that of Keyfax, of Chicago, which got under way in November 1984. Jed Laird, an analyst with Stillman Maynard, New York, explains why newspapers have stuck with videotex: "What happens is that newspaper companies are trying to assure that their current print media aren't going to be made obsolete."[6]

Yet the NAPLPS services have only attracted about 5,000 of the 30,000 customers that media analyst Link Resources predicted by 1985. Robert Bartolotta of Link now expects no more than 10,000 text-and-graphics subscribers by 1988.[7]

The biggest obstacle to success has been the cost of receiving the service. Viewtron originally required the customer to invest in a $600 AT&T videotext terminal. When this met with resistance, Viewtron tried a new approach: the terminal could be leased for $39.95 a month, which included 10 hours of free usage. Add the $12 monthly subscription fee and the dollar-an-hour fee paid to the telephone company, and the cost of home banking by Viewtron would reduce the account in the bank. Consequently, Gateway is offering an introductory price of $29.95 per month. Keyfax, which along with electronic shopping, banking and stock trading emphasizes local services, can be accessed by personal computers with about $60 worth of software. Fees for usage are $14.95 or $29.95 per month, depending on the level of service.

Videotex companies hope the cost of the service can be subsidized by advertiser revenues. But this is a familiar chicken-and-egg dilemma for developing media. Advertisers can only be attracted by a large viewer base; viewers are unlikely to subscribe to a system that costs too much because it is not yet supported by advertisers.

But the newspaper companies' difficulties have not dissuaded other big media players from getting involved. Communications giants IBM and AT&T are now staking out separate turfs. IBM has combined with CBS Inc., and Sears, Roebuck and Co. to form Trintex, which is expected to create a videotex service of its own. AT&T has responded by joining forces with Chemical Bank, Time Inc. and the Bank of America to offer its own videotex service which is also under development and is dependent upon computers for access to and display of information.[8]

The commitment by IBM and AT&T to videotex indicates that they believe the cost can be lowered and the video capability upgraded to the point where videotex will become a multibillion-dollar business. The nation's banks seem to agree. Both Chemical Bank and Bank of America offer electronic home banking for those who own personal computers. Chemical Bank's system is now in some 16,000 households, not as many as the bank had hoped but enough for it to plan going nationwide with the banking service. As Walter B. Wriston, former chief executive of Citicorp, says, "Information about money has become almost as important as money itself."[9]

VIDEOTEX AND NEWSPAPERS

When newspapers first became interested in videotex their immediate task was to determine how it would affect their newspaper business. They did this by participating in early electronic publishing efforts. Several newspapers participated in test runs that led to the introduction of Viewtron as a commercial service.[10] They learned some lessons:

- *Rapid Updating*—Videotex users expect the news to be updated even more often than it is on radio.

- *Neighborhood News*—Extremely local news, what Viewtron writers called "micronews," was very popular. This includes box scores for a local softball team, news items from individual churches, high school deadlines and reminders. Viewtron city editor Lee Ann Schlatter said, "People want to know more about what is going on in their immediate neighborhoods than the newspaper can tell them."[11]

- *Transactions*—Electronic banking and shopping were popular, but only after the user felt comfortable with the terminal.

- *Messaging*—Services that took advantage of the interactive capabilities of videotex were well received, including electronic mail.

A second major test conducted by the newspaper industry combined 11 Associated Press-member newspapers, the AP itself, and CompuServe in an electronic publishing experiment. Member newspapers provided electronic editions to CompuServe's subscribers at a cost of $5 per hour. In September 1982, AP's review of the experiment reported no "clear and present danger to the American newspaper industry from electronic delivery of information to the home—at least not in the present form of either electronic information or the newspaper industry."[12]

One could draw these important conclusions after the CompuServe test:

- *Effect on Newspaper Readership*—The availability of electronic news on CompuServe did not appear to affect traditional newspaper readership nor was radio usage diminished. Television viewing, however, dropped.

- *Value to User*—The newspaper role in the CompuServe databases was relatively minor—of all the information used, only 5% came from newspapers.

- *Potential*—The AP report said: "The potential market for electronically delivered information to the home is substantial."[13]

- *Upscale Target Market*—Those most likely to use the service were young people, those with high incomes and consumers with previous familiarity with computers. Users were definitely not representative of the general population, suggesting that at least at current price levels the potential market may not be as massive as, say, television's.

- *Telephone Use*—Consumers were worried that using their videotex service forced them to tie up their telephone. The report described this as "a formidable obstacle to broader acceptance."[14]

As interesting as the conclusions was the newspaper industry's collective sigh of relief. A reporter for *The New York Times* wrote:

> Results of the experiment . . . support the view widely held in the newspaper industry that such services are technologically feasible but that there is no mass market audience to make them profitable and thus little incentive to develop them now.[15]

That view may have been a classic case of seeing what you want to see. Certainly Lawrence Blasko, the man responsible for the AP report, made no such sweeping conclusions. He warned: "If there is advice to be found in the AP/CompuServe experiment, even if it borders on conclusion, it is that continued participation is prudent."[16]

Only 3 of the 11 newspapers chose to remain part of the CompuServe database after the experiment was over. Most concluded that the mere reformatting of general news onto a computer did not add enough value to justify the increased cost to the consumer. The newspapers that had participated in the experiment did little or no product tailoring for the videotex medium. But both CompuServe and the Viewtron trials suggested a potential market for specialized information, particularly business data, that might justify the cost of the service. In addition, the experiment found that consumers mostly use services that maximize the interactive nature of videotex: messages, banking, stock trading and so forth.

Despite the difficulties that it has encountered, the newspaper industry continues to forge ahead with videotex. Several newspapers are actively involved in public-access videotex.[17] And Gannett Co., Inc., has launched an electronic information service called "USA Today Update." It provides news and business items called "hotlines," an ASCII-type service that does not require a special terminal. The Gannett service is another example of a communications company diversifying from its existing enterprises: the news comes from *USA Today,* other Gannett newspapers and its broadcast stations.

KEY NEWSPAPER ISSUES

Having learned about videotex and, in some cases, having lost money in the business, newspaper companies must now decide where they go from here. The question is difficult because the answer depends on the company and the resources it has available. Clearly, the newspaper industry, to survive and grow as a business, must take chances and be aggressive in developing the new media that today are presenting themselves with increasing frequency. To some extent, it must develop a system of doing so. Regarding videotex, a systematic approach involves facing five fundamental issues.

To What Extent Is Videotex a Substitute for Print?

This is the question first asked by the newspaper industry, which continues to speculate that one day videotex might somehow replace print. Efrem Sigel has observed that those who advocate videotex development often do so with the unspoken conviction that it is superior to print. *Cable-Vision* magazine, for example, once posed the question, "When 1990 rolls around, will you be reading a newspaper or watching a videotext screen?"[18]

Related comments come from Claude R. Smith, president of HOMSERVE Inc., a coordinator of financial services via videotex. Smith told a UPI conference:

> Perhaps the most vulnerable medium to videotext substitution is the newspaper. Videotext timeliness and freedom from space constraints are significant competitive advantages over conventional newspapers. While newspapers in return offer portability, somewhat better graphics and no user investment, the impact on your traditional business will be certain.[19]

But looking at videotex in terms of being a replacement for print clouds thinking about the new media. Newspaper experiments in the new media tend to show that, if videotex succeeds, it will be by inventing and offering entirely new services—not recasting old ones. Legitimate similarities and differences among old and new media exist. But to understand the new media one has to advance beyond the idea that newspapers will be superseded by them (or, conversely, that newspapers do not need to respond at all). Publisher and media analyst Paul Kagan has commented: "If there is a trend toward electronic absorption of information, it has not replaced the old forms of acquiring knowledge. Indeed, it has plugged into them."[20]

Videotex Cost Versus Consumer Habits

The cost of videotex must be carefully considered, in order to determine the "highest and best use" of that particular information pipeline. It is far more expensive than print, whether the videotex system offers just text or text and graphics. For example, the 120,000-word *New York Times* costs 30 cents at the newsstand—a cost per thousand words of less than .0025 cents. Sigel has calculated what this would mean on an interactive system, as follows: *Reader's Digest's* The Source costs about $5.75 per hour with a maximum of 2000 characters per page. A reader scanning 20 complete screens in 12 minutes, at 225 words per screen, would run up a bill of $1.27 (including the $.12 telephone bill). That cost comes out to .282 cents per thousand, which makes newsprint about 110 times cheaper than an ASCII database.[21] If *The New York Times* were that expensive, the reader would pay more than $30 per issue.

The difference, of course, is that videotex is information on demand, an increasingly valuable commodity. Moreover, since 1960 virtually all forms of print communication have increased steadily in cost with little increase in readership. Electronic forms during that time have dropped in cost and grown more popular as determined by the number of words transmitted. So there is optimism that the cost of videotex will drop. One could argue the comparison is deceptive, because the true cost of newspaper information is subsidized by advertising revenue. As we have seen, however, videotex managers hope to accomplish the same. On the other hand, analysts are skeptical that the information—as opposed to the electronic hardware—will significantly drop in price. They point to the labor-intensive, expensive nature of newsgathering. It is a rising cost factor that, unlike computer chips, shows no evidence of decline.

Another cost to the videotex user must be considered: time spent changing frames. Arthur Ochs Sulzberger, publisher of *The New York Times,* calculates that a reader of his newspaper can scan up to 6000 words of information on one broadsheet page. A reader of a database would have to change screens some 27 times to access 6000 words. As Sulzberger says, "It's not a relaxing way to spend your Sunday morning."[22]

Compared to videotex, the newspaper has certain advantages besides cost. It is more portable and allows readers to scan and discard what is not of interest. Also, it is a familiar habit. Readers identify with the way they receive news. They become accustomed to their newspaper. Even as technical methods of information delivery change, the information consumer remains loyal to the old ways of learning until it is simply no longer feasible to do so. But information habits do evolve. In this century, the way people consume information has shifted radically, usually because of the introduction of new delivery systems.

Consider the habits altered by broadcasting. For the first time in history the information consumer was asked to pay for the necessary reception equipment, to share in a capital cost in order to receive a message. Little recognized is the fact that for the first 20 years of television, information consumers spent far more money to receive the signals than senders spent to transmit them. Between 1946 and 1966, consumers paid $26.5 billion for TV sets. Broadcasters spent just $1.2 billion for transmission and studio equipment. Had consumer resistance to high equipment costs been strong, it is doubtful the broadcasters could have shouldered the entire cost of a reception system. Today the average consumer spends more than $100 a year on equipment, maintenance and repair to receive "free" television. In theory, anyway, nothing prevents the consumer from paying to receive videotex.[23]

As for which product is superior, newspapers or videotex, no aspect of the information they contain necessarily differentiates them. Newspaper information can be stored on computer; computer data can be transferred to print as a very long printout. Newspapers and videotex could carry exactly the same content, leaving price and habit to decide which would prevail. But the two media naturally tend to emphasize different features. General news is too cheaply provided by established media to be the main feature of videotex, while a newspaper is not able to offer on-demand information.

In comparing the costs of different media, keep in mind what each will be used for. The concept that a given medium works well for some tasks and not so well for others is called "media relativity." Media relativity means a medium should only be judged effective or ineffective relative to the information it is supposed to carry (and, to a lesser extent, relative to the use that the information is to have). A "good medium" is one well suited to deliver the information it carries. This is why videotex may be worth the extra cost; it may prove well suited to delivering information unavailable elsewhere.

There is room in the media environment for inexpensive, general media to coexist with costly, highly specialized ones. Given sufficient incentive, consumer habits will change despite higher cost.

What Services Will Work Best on Videotex?

Early data suggest that services that capitalize on the interactive aspect of videotex have a special value to the consumer. What is so valuable about this interactive quality? If by interactive we simply mean the ability to send as well as receive information, videotex is neither the first nor the cheapest interactive system. (Those honors would go to the telephone and the postal service, respectively.) Videotex pioneers would probably say it is the speed of the computer that gives videotex its special advantage. But in an era when high-speed computers are a familiar feature on almost every office desktop, this seems an insufficient explanation of videotex's special appeal.

The difference is that videotex is the first widespread information system to use the computer to perform the actual *delivery* of information to a large audience, as opposed to information storage and processing, which computers have performed for years. When we think of videotex as computer-*delivered* information, the unique strengths of the medium become clearer:

- *Speed*—Computers react in terms of billionths of a second. They can absorb and update a tremendous amount of information at high speeds directly from other computers.

- *Storage*—Computer-based information, combined with computer-based delivery, implies a deep database available for instant information retrieval. The question then becomes: who will pay how much for instant access to a tremendous amount of what type of information?

- *User Specificity*—The computer means that mass communications can be tailored to the individual. Users can preselect an information menu and act as their own editors, opening the question of whether videotex can really be called a mass medium at all.

- *Two-Way*—The computer-based delivery system can process incoming messages as well as outgoing ones. Most of these "upstream" messages will be economic transactions or requests for information recall and electronic mail.

Accordingly, some believe mail will eventually be superseded by videotex. Certain types of electronic bulletin boards will flourish, although cost will influence their development. Business research and intelligence reports would be another potential service. A business might want to know estimates of North Sea oil production in the coming quarter; another might need to know crop conditions and weather outlook in Brazil; a third could be curious about political stability in a mineral-rich African republic. Videotex could meet such individual needs, as long as the client is willing to pay. If a newspaper had such information in its database, it could provide the service for a profit.

Videotex and computer-based information of all kinds are shaping up as the greatest research tools in history. Knowledge is expanding at an exponential rate, too much to be contained in print. More scientists, economists and engineers are alive today than in the previous 4000 years of human existence combined. Libraries are growing so fast that a Wesleyan University librarian, Fremont Rider, once calculated that by the year 2040 the Yale Library will number more than 200 million volumes and will occupy some 6000 miles of shelf space. Libraries would have to add 12 million volumes a year just to keep pace with expanding knowledge. As the educational system struggles to keep from falling behind, it will have to adopt some form of videotex/database publishing. This means added incentive to find services that work well on videotex.

Are Opportunities for Videotex Greater in the Consumer or Business Markets?

In the short run, business customers will determine how videotex develops. Computer information, some 100 times as expensive as print, limits the current consumer market in favor of business users. This cost factor will change gradually.

As costs drop, the mass consumer market becomes more attractive. But for now, the business customer calls the shots. Videotex can be an important asset, for example, to the thriving business of providing corporations with information: social forecasting, polling, consulting, consumer research and so forth.

Business can also use videotex to complete transactions. Whether a mom-and-pop store wants to sell groceries or a bank wants to sell part of its portfolio, every transaction involves policies and procedures that leave a trail of paperwork. To the extent that computers can buy, sell, transfer, calculate and so forth with extreme speed and convenience, they can speed business transactions. Banks are particularly interested in winnowing their armies of tellers through electronic banking.

What Is the Role of the Newspaper?

Each newspaper must look for opportunities appropriate to its resources. Generally speaking, newspapers must be prepared to undertake product development in their markets—introducing new types of services to their customers—or someone else will. As newspapers are not very accustomed to product development, although many are more experienced in the wake of their experiments with cable text, some newspapers will seek the help of a communications partner. But those taking this route should try to establish an understanding that will protect their role in the community. Newspapers are interested in the new media, after all, because they want to remain the central information providers in their communities.

Newspapers are already involved in videotex as information providers. Some newspapers sell the full-text version of their publications to the information supermarkets. Some newspapers have other information that they collect, process and sell for electronic distribution. These include BRS (Bibliographical Retrieval Service), the *Louisville Courier-Journal Times* abstractor. Still other newspapers opt to own the distribution system itself, such as Knight-Ridder's Vu-Text.

Newspapers can provide information about stocks, weather updates, breaking sports news and so forth. But they are also positioned to undertake specialized information-gathering for business and other clients. Newspapers should cast their information net wide. They should also seize any opportunity they have to expand into another aspect of information gathering, storage, processing and delivery.

Many advertising possibilities exist as well. Use of videotex for display advertising is likely to increase, and experimentation is already under way for classifieds. Video advertisements through videodiscs or other technology may soon be prevalent as well. Newspapers must guard against internal resistance to these new revenue opportunities as they present themselves. Newspapers that view themselves as major players in their communications environment will strive to remain the central information source in their community. By doing so, they will have a major role to play in shaping the communications environment of the future.

NOTES

1. Geert De Clercq, "Videotex," (Columbia University Graduate School of Journalism Master's Project, 1985): 5–10.

2. Walter B. Wriston, "Publishers Go Electronic," *Business Week* (June 11, 1984).

3. Efrem Sigel et al, *The Future of Videotext* (White Plains, NY: Knowledge Industry Publications, Inc., 1983), p. 1.

4. Ibid., pp. 81–111.

5. "Knight-Ridder to Fire 20% of Viewtron Staff; Poor Sales Are Cited," *Wall Street Journal* (October 31, 1984): 2.

6. De Clercq, "Videotex," p. 10.

7. Ibid.

8. Andrew Pollack, "AT&T Videotex Plan Reported," *The New York Times* (February 5, 1985): D-1.

9. Walter B. Wriston, "Publishers Go Electronic," *Business Week* (June 11, 1984).

10. Margaret Genovese, "All Eyes Are on Viewtron Screen Test," *presstime* (December 1983): 22–23.

11. Lee Ann Schlatter, "News Heard Over the Backyard Fence," *Viewtron Magazine* (December 1983): 40.

12. Jonathan Friendly, "Study Finds No Mass Market for Newspapers on Home TV," *The New York Times* (October 2, 1982): 14. Also see R. C. Morse, "Videotex in America," *Editor & Publisher* (June 26, 1982): 41-47.

13. Margaret Genovese, "AP/CompuServe Report: There's No Threat—Yet," *presstime* (October 1982): 27.

14. Ibid.

15. Jonathan Friendly, "Study Finds No Mass Market," p. 14.

16. Ibid.

17. Margaret Genovese, "Newspapers' Videotext Systems Being Tried in Shopping Malls," *presstime* (August 1983): 12. Also see Martin Lane, "Public Access Videotex," *Videotex Canada.* (Spring 1984): 17–46.

18. David Stoller, "Second Wave Videotex," *CableVision* (February 14, 1982): 57. Also see "Hackensack (N.J.) Record and CBS in Videotex Test," *Editor & Publisher* (May 15, 1982): 13.

19. Claude R. Smith, in an address at the United Press International's annual EDICON conference, Denver, CO (September–October 1982).

20. Paul Kagan, "Videotex Prospects—Hot or Not?" *Advertising Age,* (November 15, 1982): M–13.

21. Efrem Siegel, *The Future of Videotext* (White Plains, NY, Knowledge Industry Publications, Inc., 1983).

22. Arthur Ochs Sulzberger, "The New Competition," *Editor & Publisher* (May 22, 1982): 8.

23. Ben H. Bagdikian, *The Information Machines* (New York: Harper & Row, Publishers, 1971), pp. 221–23.

8

The Changing Role of Newspapers

For two hundred years, the newspaper has traditionally been the most important news medium in the communities of America. But today new competitors are infiltrating newspapers' territory, challenging them at the community level. While there is no reason to believe that either newspapers or the communities they serve will die out, naturally they will change. Both are inextricably linked; it is hard to understand one without at least mentioning the other. One would be hard-pressed to name a business that would be more adversely affected than newspapers if that evanescent feeling called "community spirit" were to ebb.

As we consider the future of newspapers, we cannot help but notice how social and technological changes in this century have altered journalism. The rise of suburbs is just one example. Metropolitan newspapers have been forced to extend themselves beyond their core cities, despite rising distribution costs. Aggressive suburban newspaper entrepreneurs have sprung up. Rural newspapers have often watched their towns evolve into bedroom communities.

Now the question is, will the rise of the new media bring similar changes? Or will changes in the way people use media leave newspapers and communities untouched? More than anything else, the answers to these questions will decide the future of newspaper journalism.

CENTRALIZATION OF MEDIA

Several trends point to a growing nationalism, or centralization, in communications. The success of national newspapers, and the growth of chains, suggest that an entire market segment is waiting to be served.

One reason for the centralization is economics of scale, to which the newspaper business has traditionally been resistant. Each newspaper has always depended on its own staff to generate local news. Therefore, the increased profitability a newspaper shows when brought into a chain usually results from better management, not savings on ink or paper. Consequently, as Compaine has pointed out, newspaper ownership is much less concentrated than that of most manufacturing businesses. To the extent a newspaper subscriber buys "community information" rather than "a newspaper," the medium resists economies of scale—because the high cost of gathering local information won't go away.[1]

The new media are different. Although often owned and even programmed or published outside of the community, they often appear to deliver information about it, or relevant to it, as with cable television. Cable's new programs and voices influence the community. People define themselves partially in terms of the programs they can get.

Cable News Network and The Weather Channel are examples of this influence. CNN, with its 24-hour coverage, uses television and the telephone to reach out to communities across the nation. During the Christmas season, for example, CNN works with the National Travelers Advisory to give viewers up-to-the-minute traffic reports about their local highways. People call into a CNN-promoted telephone number to get information.

The Weather Channel is even more impressive. It provides a unique balance of local, regional and national weather to cable systems everywhere. Cable systems electing to carry The Weather Channel receive sensing devices that allow them to report on local weather conditions, and decoding devices permit each station to receive the regional weather information for its area. Weather Channel officials say local residents learn of weather bulletins faster than if they tuned in to a local radio station.

Although possibly primitive by future standards, such systems demonstrate that local information can be distributed nationally with the use of advanced electronic equipment. What may not change is the need for locally based information gatherers—reporters.

The Power of the Computer

The computer, with its ability to process, store and deliver tremendous quantities of information tailored to specific needs, could provide the first information system based outside of the community that delivers community information on a national level.

At first this might be limited to travel data, stocks, weather and other information already stored and processed by computer. But as computer storage of information grows, more and more could be provided automatically. To the extent that such an information system is offered cheaply—not likely much before 1995—community newspapers could be forced to change the emphasis of their coverage. Newspapers fear that the community might rely on someone outside it for its local news. Of course, this contradicts fundamental notions about how our media work—newspapers have, up to now, felt secure in their special community relationship.

The Local Role in Videotex Development

In response to changing emphasis of news coverage, some community newspapers have experimented with videotex, often offering only small databases and primitive services. But their involvement shows that Fortune 500 companies have not done all the experimenting.

For example, the *Hackensack* (NJ) *Record* has contributed to the CBS/AT&T videotex venture in Ridgewood, New Jersey. The *Record* does not control the computer or the distribution facilities, but its involvement enables it to continue to put the newspaper in the forefront of local information delivery.

Newspapers attempting to carve out a local niche for videotex development should consider some guidelines.

Determine the Appropriate Investment

First, each newspaper has to determine the scale of investment appropriate for its market. Community publishers should realize the most expensive tasks must be done by major corporations, and may want to join forces with them.

New Media Test Objectives

Once the appropriate level of investment is determined, the publisher must establish test objectives. In other words, what does the publisher hope to accomplish through experimentation with the new media?

These objectives should be drafted during the earliest stages of the project, and should be realistic. For example, a publisher might say:

> We're experimenting with videotex so that we can later market a videotex system better than Telidon.

But this goal is unrealistic for all but a few newspaper corporations.

The objective should also be as specific as possible. A goal entitled "developing third wave communications technologies in our market" sounds nice,

but does not mean much. The objectives must be narrow enough for the newspaper to use them later to determine the success or failure of the project.
One possible set of objectives:

1. We want to assess the costs of operating a full blown system in our market.

2. We want to find out what types of people are likely to be interested in the service.

3. We want to learn what types of information, provided electronically, will be of interest.

4. We want to determine three options we might pursue for future new media involvement.

Types of Ventures

The corporate organization of a project may take several forms. The newspaper could decide to go it alone or to try a joint venture. Teaming up with a larger partner can often minimize risk, and reduce both expense and relative control. The newspaper wants to guard its predominant role in the community zealously.

New forms of communications are being developed every year. Newspapers cannot stop them from affecting the community. But the newspaper can get involved and help with the direction of them. As partners in ventures, newspapers should work to preserve the integrity of the local communications marketplace and call upon new communications firms entering the local community to abide by the following standards:

1. *Editorial Independence*—The newspaper will never compromise its editorial independence for any reason.

2. *Editorial Control*—The newspaper company must have final editorial control over any information that will be identified with the newspaper. This does not mean the newspaper should be permitted the right of review for non-newspaper parts of the information system, only those that bear its name. The newspaper, of course, reserves its right to withdraw its participation, if overall content is contrary to the community's tastes.

3. *Technology Transfer*—The newspaper should obtain an agreement permitting maximum transfer of test information, including technol-

ogy, to the newspaper. This could include an option to buy any equipment that might be left behind after the experiment's conclusion. A clause allowing newspaper participation in other technologies brought into the market, by the partner or anyone else, is desirable. Also, the other partner should supply any needed technical assistance to the newspaper, which should concentrate on providing editorial and advertising content.

4. *Newspaper Prominence—*The newspaper should be visibly in the driver's seat in the new media venture and should work to achieve this image. After all, the point of being involved is to enhance the newspaper's position. The newspaper is a familiar and trusted entity, and high visibility will help the newspaper to maintain prominence.

5. *Printing Agreement—*The newspaper should work for an arrangement to handle any printing work generated by the new media test, at competitive rates. This will avoid a TV guide that is neither owned nor printed by the newspaper.

6 *Marketing—*The newspaper should market the new media system to its clients. You do not want a newcomer visiting your clients to discuss advertising.

7. *Indemnification—*Both companies, for liability purposes, should indemnify the other for any damages, suits, etc., that might occur.

8. *Equity—*The newspaper company should have *an option for equity* in the venture, should it later choose to buy in. This will tend to maximize the transfer of technology mentioned above in Standard 3. But the newspaper must carefully review conflict-of-interest and antitrust considerations before it exercises its option.

Newspapers as New Media Partners

Of course, newspapers must be able to offer something in return. Each newspaper should carefully assess what it has to bring to the new media partnership.

The newspaper's obvious strength is its predominance in the local information market. Hundreds of customers reach the newspaper's audience through advertising. For a new business seeking credibility and acceptance, the newspaper's audience is of great value. Through it, the newspaper will be able to introduce the new product to the community effectively. One approach might require marketing personnel to plan an advertising campaign.

Another advantage newspapers offer is their printing plant. The newspaper should aggressively seek any printing business associated with the new venture so no apparently harmless TV guide will evolve into a print competitor.

Newspapers also have information to sell and have expertise in gathering information locally. Why not collect information for the new media business as well?

Giving the Store Away?

But if newspapers have so much to offer, do they risk giving away the store by helping the newcomer gain a local foothold?

The question may be moot. Whether newspapers help the new media, the latter will grow and develop. We are moving from an era of media scarcity to media diversity. All media are no longer mass. It is better for newspapers to adapt to changing conditions than to fight them. However, most newspapers will not have the resources or the experienced staff to develop the new media on their own. Joint ventures limit risk in a risky business.

Too many pathways to the local market exist for the newspaper to control them all. The challenge is to take advantage of the newspaper's existing position to sell information and advertising via as many systems as possible. The danger lies in ignoring this new direction in communications.

Thanks to the computer, proximity no longer determines appeal to a given market. The new media have combined elements of near and far in a way that is just beginning to become apparent. The community newspaper has a vital role as a gatekeeper to the local community, introducing changes to people where they live. No institution is better suited than the newspaper to achieve this.

EFFECTS OF NEWSPAPER INVOLVEMENT

Involvement in the new media has emancipated newspapers from a host of assumptions about their business. Managers are viewing their jobs differently and becoming more willing to innovate.

As the year 2000 looms, newspaper people are wondering what the newspaper of the future will look like, who its readers will be, how its newsrooms will operate and what skills its journalists will need.

Such farsighted questions demonstrate the vitality of the newspaper business: "Ten years ago, the thought of a newspaper becoming involved in cable as an 'electronic newspaper' seemed to many to be almost sacrilegious. The two were thought of as being incompatible at best, and as bloody competitors at worst."[2]

That transition behind them, newspapers today are more flexible than ever before. Responding to the changing needs of advertisers and readers, newspapers are exploring new ideas that would have seemed farfetched only a few years ago. Some of these follow.

Tiering

Tiering means dividing a product into its parts so that the consumer pays only for what he needs. Telephone companies have used tiering successfully for decades. Their service includes a basic charge, an equipment rental charge, a local service charge based on units used and a long-distance charge. The consumer pays for the tiers of service that apply. Similarly, cable companies offer basic service, an additional fee for extra TV hookups and a charge for each movie service.

Newspapers operate on a different pricing system: the comprehensive package. As newspapers are designed to provide many different types of information, regardless of the costs of gathering them, sometimes news of interest to a fraction of the public is omitted in favor of an item of wider appeal.

Today, newspaper managers speak of "unbundling," or tiering the newspaper product. They want to target special sections to those who want that information. The newspaper might charge separately for these, and further specialize the news content.

> We don't believe [says *Newsday* publisher David Laventhol] that the newspaper in the Year 2000 will be exactly the same as it is now. Some of the electronic experimentation could result in a video offshoot of the newspaper, for example—service material like stocks, box scores, and weather data might be available on electronic subsidiaries, and classified ads might access easily on a call-up home system.[3]

Tiering the newspaper means the final product must be more closely tailored to the needs of individual consumers—both the readers and the advertisers. But newspapers should proceed with utmost care before dismantling their print publication. Perhaps tiered pricing should apply only to new services offered by the newspaper, rather than the unbundling of existing sections.

Tiered pricing requires a complex distribution network to get the right information to the right consumer. When cable companies tier movie channels, they control distribution with a series of programmable converters, or signal trap devices. This ensures the integrity of their tier structure. Similarly, the newspaper's complex marketing goals must be supported by effective distribution methods.

The Enhanced Distribution Network

Newspapers are beginning to use computers to enhance their distribution system. Challenged by direct mail, they are collecting nonsubscriber lists. *Newsday*, for example, distributes a total market coverage publication of about 30 pages of ads. It is available once a week to 300,000 nonsubscriber households on Long Island.

Coupled with the new distribution capacity of the computer is a reevaluation of the "13-year-old brigade" that delivers our newspapers each day. In Ben Compaine's book, *The Newspaper Industry in the 1980s*, the author cites an ANPA survey that found that delivery problems are the leading reason for subscription cancellations. Accordingly, newspapers are taking another look at their delivery systems. The *Los Angeles Times*, for example, has replaced its independent carrier system with a network of 200 full-time and 1000 part-time workers. They collect money, deliver papers, manage carriers and the like. The start-up cost was $4 million, with associated costs of about $27 million. The shift resulted in an additional $23 million in circulation revenue in its first year.[4]

Publishing the Database

Another new idea is to publish more of the information the newspaper gathers. This publication might be electronic. Only about a tenth of all the information collected by reporters is ever actually published. Why not format the rest to appeal to special audiences?

Suppose, for example, the local board of supervisors receives a 200-page report on economic development. A 1200-word article is published. Yet many in the community—bankers, lawyers, developers, real estate agents, involved citizens—might be willing to pay up to $25 for the original report.

Jon G. Udell discussed the concept in *The Economics of the American Newspaper*:

> Looking to the twenty-first century, newspapers will be marketing a wide variety of information which they now discard. This will take several different forms. Each day a newspaper receives many times as much information as it can publish. In the future, news from wire services will be digitally encoded in computers, ready for manipulation into packages of data useful to special interest groups.[5]

The growing popularity of home computers could spur this database movement. The director of Gannett's New Media Task Force, Lawrence R. Fuller, has said, "My vision is that by 1990, based on what our research indicates, between 30% and 50% of the homes will have personal computers and that the majority of those personal computers will have modems (to allow reception of messages by phone)."[6] In other words, newspapers should not wait until the arrival of videotex to consider database publishing.

Media Versatility

A corollary of database publishing is media versatility. Increasingly, publishers see other media as part of the same process that ends up with a newspaper thrown on the doorstep. New media are increasingly important sources of news, a point that encourages media diversity in the way newspapers gather and distribute it. As long as managers do not somehow compromise the newspaper's position, they should try to use other media, at least for newsgathering purposes. Why not have a newspaper talk show on radio or report sports scores on community television?

Media versatility would work well for the newspaper's advertisers also. One stop at the newspaper's marketing office and they could buy direct mail, TMC (Total Market Coverage), newspaper advertising, cable advertising, LPTV, teletext or others. The newspaper could offer a comprehensive package to the client, giving the newspaper tremendous leverage to cross-promote its services from one medium to the next. This cross-promotion would solidify the newspaper's position as the community's main information provider. One caveat: publishing a newspaper remains the anchor business of the media-versatile publisher. Modernization must occur from the inside out and should not overlook needed improvements in printing equipment.

It is clear, then, that the newspaper business is now experiencing two significant, historic changes. It is evolving into a community information center, and from a manufacturing to a service business.

The Community Information Center

An information center offers a host of services. These include direct mail, community television, cable and more. Its comprehensive nature means it becomes the chief marketing expert on the local or regional level. Because a great deal of revenue comes from marketing services, advertising representatives become marketing consultants.

The information center is a one-stop shop, where you can buy any information you need in a given community. It is a nexus for news, a place where information automatically flows. And it is an efficient marketing system, with a highly capable team fulfilling the marketing objectives of management, rather than a number of individuals working to boost their commission checks.

The Newspaper Service Industry

Newspapers want to be the sole, or at least the chief, source of news and advertising. To do so, they must offer clients:

- marketing plan development
- time buying
- media referral
- information delivery
- public relations planning
- advertising production
- promotion and special events

It is no coincidence that these are service-oriented jobs. Traditionally newspapers have used heavy machinery (presses) to accomplish a rote production process (printing) to create an item for sale, the newspaper. The newspaper industry has been a manufacturing business.

Often without realizing it, newspaper people have discussed their business in manufacturing terms: units produced, units sold, cost per page of production, work hours per page, inventory (news hole), production schedules (deadlines), and so on. The jargon of the news business is defined by the printing press: upper and lower case, leading out, picas, hot and cold type, and so forth.

Economists believe manufacturing businesses tend to have common characteristics: high fixed assets and low variable costs. Return on investment is constrained by high cost of fixed assets, even when revenues are large, prompting an ongoing effort to increase efficiency and reduce costs. This is common in the newspaper business. One time-honored book on newspaper management, published in the 1950s, advised: "Double the life of carbon paper by passing used carbon paper over a steam pipe, with the carbon side to the heat. The carbon melts and is distributed equally over the surface."[7]

The emphasis on streamlining existing operations is now changing. Dollars saved by forgoing a TMC (Total Market Coverage) product or a direct-mail list may actually cost money in the long run, because of an increasingly competitive communications environment. The path to profitability has grown riskier and more complex. Efficiency alone does not address more fundamental marketing questions.

It is time for newspapers to concentrate on fundamental competitive issues: product differentiation, consumer habits, market share, home penetration, new opportunities, changing characteristics of local markets and others. This shift in emphasis leaves manufacturing concepts less important to newspapers, while service functions—marketing and planning—assume a greater role. As a service business, the newspaper can afford lower gross revenues and still achieve a high return on investment. It will be more flexible to future changes, because less of the business will be tied to heavy machinery.

Edwin Emery notes that there is an "ever-increasing attention to audience and motivational research, readership and listenership studies, readability formulas, and design and layout. Some dailies have employed their own research directors."[8]

The new relationship of the newspaper with its community, along with tiering, the enhanced distribution network, database publishing and media versatility, are all offspring of the new media environment.

NOTES

1. Benjamin M. Compaine, *The Newspaper Industry in the 1980s* (White Plains, NY: Knowledge Industry Publications, Inc., 1980), pp. 85–111.

2. "Member Involvement in Cable: Wave of the Future?" *Suburban Publisher* (February 1982): 1.

3. David Laventhol, "Communications Revolution," in an address before the *Business Week* magazine conference on confronting the communications revolution, New York City, (June 8, 1982).

4. Benjamin M. Compaine, *The Newspaper Industry in the 1980s* (White Plains, NY: Knowledge Industry Publications, Inc., 1982), p. 41.

5. Jon G. Udell, *The Economics of the American Newspaper* (New York: Hastings House, 1978), p. 151.

6. Margaret Genovese, "PCs No Longer Seen as a Threat," *presstime* (June 1984): 20. Also see "Papers enter PC field," *presstime* (June 1984): 19.

7. Frank W. Rucker and Herbert Lee Williams, *Newspaper Organization and Management* (Iowa: Iowa State University Press, 1955), p. 135.

8. Edwin Emery, *The Press and America* (Englewood Cliffs, N.J.: Prentice-Hall, Inc., 1972), p. 732.

9

Technology and the Journalist

Many newspaper reporters and managers doubt their jobs will change much because of technology, feeling that it will merely offer them new ways to express their thoughts. Even as they report on changes in society, reporters often seem indifferent to changes in their own profession.

But the fact remains that journalists rely on tools, at least a pencil and a pad of paper, to do their jobs. Without basic technology, there would be no journalism, which has never been independent of the processes used to accomplish it.

Journalists must appreciate that the tools of the trade help define the trade, and that technology and journalism principles are related. Probably the printer-editors who founded American journalism—the Franklins, Benjamin Harris, the Bradfords—had a better sense of this than our modern reporters do.

Today, the most obvious example of the importance of new technology is the video display terminal (VDT), which shifts typesetting responsibilities to the newsroom. The journalist may think of a VDT as an enhanced typewriter, but its historical significance goes far beyond that: it involves the journalist in production once again.

Today, whole categories of journalistic endeavor can be traced to technology. National newspapers, for example, are possible because of the advances in satellite communications. Journalists on the campaign trail use small personal computers to file stories back home.[1] Microwave links facilitate use of remote printing plants. And leagues of reporters work for publications that cover specialized technologies.

As this relationship between the journalist and the technical means of gathering and reporting information emerges, we see a new breed of communicator, the technojournalist. In reporting, working and thinking, the journalist of the future will be different from those of today. The journalist of the future will have to balance the humanistic sensitivity that produces the best journalism with newfound technological tools. Journalists must not settle for becoming mere scientists' apprentices; they will have to look at the impact of technology on values.

THE INFORMATION TECHNICIAN

The technojournalist of the future will be plugged into myriad information sources, some routine and others exotic. Multiply the present information flow by a hundred, and you begin to approach the information load of the future. New tools and methods will be needed to handle this avalanche.

The technojournalist will have to become an information technician, using new information tools and information management techniques. The training of journalists will have to be different. New concepts will be needed to help newspaper managers decide what information deserves priority treatment. Anyone who has watched a young editor struggle to establish information priorities must wonder if the newspaper of the future will be able to limit itself to OJT (on-the-job training). An information technician will have to be taught to recognize and react to information dysfunction—when one can no longer handle information effectively because of overload.

In the future, the mass-media journalist may be the exception rather than the rule. The journalist will have to gain a deeper, more diverse understanding of communication, largely because of the way information will be stored—in databases.

Database Journalism

The technojournalist will sometimes flit from database to database with the flick of a finger, probing electronically into the most labyrinthine passageways of government and industry. Adroit in navigating such mazes, the journalist will gain access to astonishing sources of detailed information—information that corporate and government authorities may find embarrassing. New efforts to restrict First Amendment freedom will inevitably result.

Will the journalist risk being co-opted by an information elite? In an age when access to information is a path to power, journalists might be tempted to forget that their job is to serve the public. Technojournalists will have to mediate between these elites and the rest of society. They will have to master the techniques of the new media elite in order to challenge it effectively when necessary. Yet the journalist will have to develop unofficial information sources as well.

Database journalism sounds futuristic, but it is not. Already, much of today's journalism involves culling vast databanks. The School of Journalism at the University of Western Ontario has studied more than 1000 publicly accessible databases now in North America. "Journalists have used databanks for years," comments Professor Henry Overduin. "What is new and novel about Newsdat [a University of Western Ontario project] is that it represents the first systematic attempt to use information stored in databanks as a prime source of news."[2]

Database journalism says a great deal about where our reporting is headed. With tremendous amounts of information being generated by government, emphasis may shift from gathering data to analyzing, by computer, information collected by others.[3] Computer use may even affect writing styles. One videotex page producer observed: "There is a tendency for messages to be tighter, more condensed and less redundant."[4]

Media Versatility and Specialization

With the advent of technology will come media-versatile journalists. The strict division between video and print media journalists will fade, to be replaced by those capable of handling different forms. But even as they become media-versatile, journalists will tend to become subject specialists. Up to now, our concept of journalists has been shaped by the needs of the mass media, a haven for the journalistic generalist. We assume this is what a journalist should be, but the new media represent the first change in this assumption.

Already the trade press has expanded, and there is an increasing number of specialty magazines and other specialty publications. The new media will allow the journalist to break free from the mass audience in pursuit of special subjects. But the specialist risks being mesmerized by technical language and losing touch with the audience. Our language is growing more complex, more arcane. Acronyms and neologisms sprout around us: 11,000 words were added to the *Webster's New Collegiate Dictionary* between its eight and ninth editions. This complicates the communicator's task. But with care, the journalistic specialist will be in better touch with a new, more precisely defined audience.

The specialist will mediate between highly technical audiences and a somewhat broader public. But the specialists will not displace the existing mass media, which will continue—if only because at some point the efficiency of placing an advertising message before a mass audience will substitute for that of placing a highly specialized advertising message before select audiences. However, to the extent that mass media audiences are breaking up, going their own way, and aggressively selecting their own information, our communications environment will have to change as well.

Story Verification

Along with specialization will come an increasing number of stories written by free-lancers who have a particular expertise. The use of free-lance material will aggravate the growing credibility problems facing our media. The devastating effect of the Janet Cooke fabrication on the *Washington Post* is just one example that points out the urgency of taking new steps to verify stories.

In the future, free-lancers and perhaps even regular staffers may voluntarily seek a professional rating through the ANPA or some other organization, such as the American Press Institute, to establish their reliability. The rating might be determined by careful examination of a writer's work by fact-checkers and other journalists, and would be available to editors. Although most journalists would probably oppose even the sort of intra-professional rating scale discussed here, newspapers need to protect themselves from flagrant fabrications. In order to do so, they should treat their reporters as professionals—which many do not do—and should expect professional standards from them. Furthermore, we should not deceive ourselves by thinking that reporters are necessarily more moral than the rest of us.

Newspapers may also hire fact-checkers. A proper balance must be struck between skepticism and creativity, but in an information-oriented society, credibility will be paramount. Again, technology will play a role, as an increasing amount of fact-checking will be done by computer. The computer will perform two types of checks: an internal check to examine spelling, punctuation, usage and facts asserted implicitly within the story itself; and a check of external facts to verify the background of the story. This will catch misspellings, incorrect dates and place names, and so forth.

The software to verify facts by computer does not exist yet, but it is on the way. For example, Bell Laboratories has developed a 32-program computer system called "Writer's Workbench," which analyzes news stories for common writing ptifalls: use of passives, nominalizations, use of "which" instead of "that" for restrictive clauses, poor diction, split information, awkward sentence structures and monotonous sentences. Also, it summarizes average sentence length, average word length and the percentage of simple sentences. An even deeper analysis of text may come from the International Business Machines's EPISTLE copy-editing system, which reportedly is capable of making some semantic distinctions.[5]

One final consideration: if, on the other hand, we print only stories that have been scrutinized by an army of attorneys, editors and fact-checkers, do we not risk losing some creativity in the process?

Backgrounders

These specialists of the future will add context to newspaper stories. As events occur faster, they become less meaningful unless put in historical context.[6]

New Staff

Machines, of course, will not do all the work. Researchers will be needed, experts in database journalism. They may spend little time actually reporting, but they will be fluent in computer information systems and languages. They will be able to draw information from databases.

Similarly, experts will be needed to interpret the information. The use of graphs, charts, visual aids and other devices will be elevated to an art. The explainers will learn the best way to describe a complex event or thought to a layperson.

Someone will also have to explain the new equipment and processes being developed all the time. Just as many newspapers employ a writing coach, communications companies of the future may need a technology coach, who will prepare journalists for greater changes to come, and will help train them in new systems.

Decentralization of Editorial Functions

At present, many of these journalism jobs are already performed by the newspaper's editor, which suggests the next change for newspapers will be the decentralization of the editorial functions. Increasingly, these chores will move to specialists who operate under the editor's supervision, which will free the editor to concentrate on creative tasks, such as improving the overall information product.

Decentralization does not mean the editor's role will be diluted. In an era when newspaper growth depends on offering finely tuned information products, the editor becomes more important than ever, and, thanks to the computer, the editor will have more creative control. Accordingly, the editor will gradually evolve into more of an information executive who delegates and maintains quality control after establishing the goals, tone and style of the publication.

The tremendous volume of information being generated makes this decentralization necessary. Unless lower levels of staff weed it out, editors will be unable to cope. Also, the development of new information systems, operated by specialists, leads to decentralization. In an information-oriented society, the editor is forced to rely on a decentralized structure of experts, specialists and the technojournalist. Finally, decentralization results, ironically, from the need for greater quality control. The editor must be free to be creative—too many have to spend their time just trying to meet deadlines.

DISCRETE NEWSGATHERING

Overreliance on the telephone is considered a problem for today's journalist. But consider the world of the technojournalist, whose electronic news sources are many times more powerful. But they are also farther removed from where the news actually occurs.

The journalist of the future might write a detailed background story on a candidate, complete with quotes, voting record, political ideology, family background and so on . . . all without talking to a single source, by phone or otherwise. This might be accomplished many times faster by computer than through library research.

But the distant, discrete quality of this information has weaknesses. At some point, when a journalist is removed from direct contact with the source of a story, accuracy suffers, nuance is lost, unexpected information is harder to turn up, and rapport with the source, which leads to new tips in the future, can be harder to establish.

Journalists must be careful about the powerful new information tools they wield. Guidelines should be established for source citation, for personal interviews and for which types of stories allow for computer use and which do not.

A certainty: disinformation, trickery, mistakes, and outright lies will occur no less often on electronic systems than before. The difference is they will do more damage, with errors echoing throughout the system until the electronic correction catches up. While some stories will come from electronically stored information, the journalist will have to journey out of his electronic workshop to get a feel for sources' personalities and to build relationships. The alternative is a journalism highly subject to manipulation.

THE WORLD OF THE FUTURE JOURNALIST

Journalists, as always, will be affected by major trends, and the primary trend we face is the shift toward an information society. Exactly what this shift means has confused a decade of technocrats, futurists and social scientists. But it is likely to make the journalist's work more important than ever. The journalist will trade in the most valuable coin in the realm: credible information.

Uncertainties accompany this opportunity. The journalist must decide whether to serve mass or specialized audiences. Newspapers must take risks to capitalize on the opportunities ahead.[7]

The second important trend is toward a world society of rapid change. Information is the one commodity that, upon being consumed, does not decrease the total supply. Rather, the process feeds on itself. New ideas generate more new ideas. With the mass media, the variety of available information could not be fully communicated. The new media, adding a wealth of information pathways to and from the individual, bring information pluralism.

Just as new ideas bring change, forcing people to adjust, the tools that people use to do their work will change also. John Naisbitt writes:

> Yes, the most formidable challenge will be to train people to work in the information society. Jobs will become available, but who will possess the high-tech skills to fill them? Not today's graduates who cannot manage simple arithmetic or write basic English.[8]

Journalists must realize their tools are changing. Once they master them, they will become technojournalists, relying on technical systems and methods to do their jobs. Similarly, the organizations employing these journalists are changing also. Some will call upon the journalist to specialize. New journalistic jobs will emerge, both in and out of the newsroom, as newspapers attempt to deal with information in a more systematic, more sophisticated manner. Even the timeless editorial values of objectivity and humanism may be challenged and possibly modified. The journalists of the future will be expected to give traditional journalistic values and concepts new interpretations, and to apply them to new situations.

At the same time that journalists respond to change, of course they must not overreact. They have to overcome "techno-doom"—the feeling of helplessness in the face of accelerating change.[9] By recognizing change, by preparing for it and eventually by meeting it aggressively rather than reacting to it, journalists will be more effective than ever before.

NOTES

1. Peter Brown, "Model 100 Proof," *Washington Journalism Review* (July/August 1984): 9.

2. Henry Overduin, "J-School to Probe Newsroom Databanks," *Editor & Publisher* (January 22, 1983): 36.

3. Leonard Downie, Jr., *The New Muckrakers* (Washington, D.C.: New Republic Book Company, Inc., 1976), pp. 93–111.

4. Barbara J. Weiss, "Writing for Videotex," *Videotex Canada* (Fall 1983): 14–21.

5. Mark Holt, "Computer-Editor Can Talk Back," *Publisher's Auxiliary* (September 28, 1981): 3.

6. David Haughey, "The News Library: A Key to Future Market Dominance," *Editor & Publisher* (June 25, 1983): 33. Haughey writes "The key is to provide more than what a few reporters can provide, to go beyond current news and to allow access to past information as well."

7. John Morton, "Journalism Doesn't Pay," *Washington Journalism Review* (July/August 1984): 15.

8. John Naisbitt, *Megatrends* (New York: Warner Books, Inc., 1982), p. 250.

9. "Techno-doom talk," *Editor & Publisher* (March 26, 1983): 6.

Bibliography

Abbott, Sharon. "Newspapers and Cable TV." Address to the American Press Institute's "Newspapers, Telecommunications and Cable TV" Seminar, September 1982, at Reston, VA.

Anderson, Robert L. "Newspapers and Cable TV." Address to the American Press Institute's "Newspapers, Telecommunications and Cable TV" Seminar, September 1982, at Reston, VA.

ANPA report: "Low Power Television Marketing Considerations." ANPA information packet prepared by the ANPA Department of Telecommunications Affairs.

Armstrong, David. *A Trumpet to Arms, Alternative Media in America.* Boston, MA: South End Press, 1981.

Arundel, Arthur W. Address to the Suburban Newspapers of America (SNA) Cable TV Seminar, October 1981, at Airlie, VA.

Ashcraft, Mark F. "Newspaper Cable: Why Should You Be Interested?" Address to the South Carolina Press Association, February 1981, at Greenville, SC.

Bagdikian, Ben H. *The Information Machines.* New York: Harper & Row, Publishers, 1971.

Bogart, Leo. "Media and a Changing America," *Advertising Age* (March 29, 1982).

Bortz, Paul. "Consultant's Caveat: Don't Forget the Basics," *Electronic Publisher* (March 10, 1982).

Brown, Merrill. "CBS Shows How to Fail With Cable," *Washington Post* (September 16, 1982).

Brown, Peter. "Model 100 Proof," *Washington Journalism Review* (July-August 1984).

Burgoon, Judee K. et al. "What Is News? Who Decides? And How?" Preliminary report conducted for the American Society of Newspaper Editors, May 1982.

Burkhardt, F. W. "Electronic Media—An Overview," *IFRA New Media Report* 10(1984).

Christopher, Maurine. "New Cable Acceptance Shown," *Cable Marketing* (April 1982).

Compaine, Benjamin M. *The Newspaper Industry in the 1980s*. White Plains, NY: Knowledge Industry Publications, Inc., 1980.

Compaine, Benjamin M. et al. *Who Owns the Media?* White Plains, NY: Knowledge Industry Publications, Inc., 1982.

Criner, Kathleen, and Raymond B. Gallagher. "Newspaper Cable TV Services: Current Activities in Channel Leasing and Other Local Service Ventures," Report by the ANPA, March 1982.

Criner, Kathleen, and Jane Wilson. "New-technology Players Jockey for Position," *presstime* (November 1984).

Crowley, Thomas A. "Newspaper Strategies in the Developing Marketplace." Address to the American Press Institute's "Newspapers, Telecommunications and Cable TV" Seminar, September 1982, at Reston, VA.

De Clercq, Geert. "Videotex." Master's Project, Columbia University Graduate School of Journalism, 1985.

de Sola Pool, Ithiel. *The Technologies of Freedom*. Cambridge, MA: Belknap Press, 1983.

Doerken, Bill. "Vo-Tech Center Produced Cable TV News," *National High School Broadcasters Newsletter* 5 (August 1982).

Downie, Leonard, Jr. *The New Muckrakers.* Washington, DC: New Republic Book Company, Inc., 1976.

Effros, Steven. "How to Get into Cable and Channel Leasing in Multiple Franchise Areas." Address to the Suburban Newspapers of America (SNA) Cable TV Seminar, October 1981, at Airlie, VA.

Emery, Edwin. *The Press and America.* Englewood Cliffs, NJ: Prentice-Hall, Inc., 1972.

Epstein, Edward Jay. *News from Nowhere.* New York: Random House, 1973.

Fang, Irving E. *Television News, Radio News.* Champlin, MN: Rada Press, 1980.

Friendly, Jonathan. "Study Finds No Mass Market for Newspapers on Home TV," *The New York Times* (October 2, 1982).

Garneau, George. "Reporters Getting to Test Mobile Cellular Phones," *Editor & Publisher* (February 9, 1985).

Genovese, Margaret. "AP/Compu Serve report: There's no threat—yet," *presstime* (October 1982).

—— "All Eyes Are on Viewtron Screen Test," *presstime* (December 1983).

—— "Cabletelevision Market Is Still Hot, But Some Papers Get Cold Shoulder," *presstime* (April 1982).

—— "Newspapers' Videotext Systems Being Tied in Shopping Malls," *presstime* (August 1983).

—— "PCs No Longer Seen as a Threat," *presstime* (June 1984).

Graham, Katharine. Address to the New England Newspaper Association, February 1982.

—— "Graham: 'We Are Not Ready for the Obit Page,'" *Publishers' Auxiliary* (May 3, 1982).

Gruson, Sydney. "The New Competition," *Editor & Publisher* (May 22, 1982).

Haughey, David. "The News Library: A Key to Future Market Dominance," *Editor & Publisher* (June 25, 1983).

Holder, Dennis. "Cablemania," *Washington Journalism Review* (September 1982).

Hollis, Sallie Rose. "Channels Answer Interactive Call," *Advertising Age* (May 30, 1985).

Holt, Mark. "Computer-editor Can Talk Back," *Publishers' Auxiliary* (September 28, 1981).

Kaatz, Ronald B. *Cable: An Advertiser's Guide to the New Electronic Media.* Chicago: Crain Books, 1982.

Kagan, Paul. "Videotex Prospects—Hot or Not?" *Advertising Age* (November 15, 1982).

Kahaner, Larry. "Hello Sweetheart, Forget Rewrite, Get Me the Computer!" *Washington Journalism Review* (December 1981).

——— "Parting Words," *CableVision* (January 11, 1982).

Lane, Martin. "Public Access Videotex," *Videotex Canada* (Spring 1984).

Laventhol, David. "Communications Revolution." Address given at the *Business Week* magazine conference on confronting the communications revolution, June 1982.

Livingston, Victor. "A Medium of Choice," *CableVision* (August 23, 1982).

Marbut, Robert. "Publishers Ask Congress to Apply Brakes on AT&T," *Editor & Publisher* (March 20, 1982).

McHale, John. *The Changing Information Environment.* Boulder, CO: Westview Press, Inc., 1976.

Miller, Tim. "The Database as Reportorial Resource." *Editor & Publisher* (April 28, 1984).

Moozakis, Chuck. "Local Advertisers: Why We Use Cable," *TVC Magazine* (July 15, 1982).

Morse, R. C. "Videotex in America," *Editor & Publisher* (June 26, 1982).

Morton, John. "Circulation: A Household Number," *Washington Journalism Review* (June 1984).

—— "Closing In, Suburbans Increase Pressure on Metros," *Publishers' Auxiliary* (May 17, 1982).

—— "The Growth Factors," *Washington Journalism Review* (May 1984).

—— "Journalism Doesn't Pay," *Washington Journalism Review* (July-August 1984).

—— "Knight-Ridder to Fire 20% of Viewtron Staff; Poor Sales Are Cited," *Wall Street Journal* (October 31, 1984).

Munsinger, Jeff. "Publisher Changes Channels on Cable Plans," Virginia Press Association Management File, *Missouri Press News* (October 1981).

Naisbitt, John. *Megatrends.* New York: Warner Books, Inc., 1982.

Neustadt, Richard M. *The Birth of Electronic Publishing.* White Plains, NY: Knowledge Industry Publications, Inc., 1982.

Noble, J. Kendrick, Jr. "Four Expert Views." *presstime* (January 1985).

Overduin, Henry. "J-School to Probe Newsroom Databanks," *Editor & Publisher* (January 22, 1983).

Piacente, Steve. "Parting Words," *CableVision* (May 10, 1982).

Pollack, Andrew. "AT&T Videotex Plan Reported," *The New York Times* (February 5, 1985).

Poltrack, David F. "The Road to 1990: Half-Way Home." CBS/Broadcast Group report, October 1985, available from CBS Inc.

Power, Phillip H. "The Newspaper's View of Cable." Address to the Suburban Newspapers of America (SNA) Cable TV Seminar, October 1981, at Airlie, VA.

Prendergast, Joseph E., Jr. "Newspapers at Mid-Decade and Beyond—News-print," *presstime* (January 1985).

Radolf, Andrew. "Gannett papers ready for Cable TV services," *Editor & Publisher* (May 15, 1982).

—— "Newspapers See Riches in Mobile Phones," *Editor & Publisher* (June 15, 1982).

Rambo, David. "New Services Stir Variety of Questions on Marketing," *presstime* (October 1981).

Ray, Garrett. "Love Song to a Linotype," *SCAN* (Vol. 30, No. 2).

Reed, Robert. "Falling 'Star' Bad Sign for Newspapers," *Advertising Age* (March 29, 1982).

Renfroe, Patricia F., and Kathleen Criner. "How to Hire Staff for Electronic Publishing Ventures," *presstime* (January 1982).

Rickerson, Orville. Report to the First LPTV Conference, February 1982.

Rockmore, Milt. "View from the Top," *Editor & Publisher* (May 1, 1982).

Rucker, Frank W., and Herbert Lee Williams. *Newspaper Organization and Management.* Ames, IA: Iowa State University Press, 1955.

Savino, Frank J., and Thurman R. Pierce, Jr. "What's the Better Strategy: Survive or Seek Growth?" *presstime* (July 1981).

Schlatter, Lee Ann. "News Heard Over the Backyard Fence," *Viewtron Magazine* (December 1983).

Schneider, Mark D. "Cellular Communications Service: Wireline Delivery or Delay?" *Georgetown Law Journal* 72 (1984).

Schwartz, Barry N., ed. *Human Connection and the New Media.* Englewood Cliffs, NJ: Prentice-Hall, Inc., 1973.

Shaw, David. *Journalism Today: A Changing Press for a Changing America.* New York: Harper's College Press, 1977.

Siemering, Art. "A Marriage of Convenience," *Advertising Age* (April 5, 1982).

Sigel, Efrem et al. *The Future of Videotext.* White Plains, NY: Knowledge Industry Publications, Inc., 1983.

Slowthrower, David W. "Sears Exec Warns Newspapers of Impending Linage Losses," *Editor & Publisher* (February 6, 1982).

Smith, Bev. "VU/TEXT—Newspaper 'Morgue' Reincarnated as Online Vendor," *Information Today* (October 1984).

Smith, Claude R. Address given at the United Press International's (UPI) Annual EDICON Conference, September-October 1982.

Smith, Ralph Lee. *The Wired Nation.* New York: Harper & Row, Publishers, 1972.

Stoller, David. "Second Wave Videotex," *CableVision* (February 14, 1982).

Strange, William B., Jr. "Economics of the Cable Industry—Advertising and Cable." Address to the Suburban Newspapers of America (SNA) Cable TV Seminar, October 1981, at Airlie, VA.

Sulzberger, Arthur Ochs. "The New Competition," *Editor & Publisher* (May 22, 1982).

Tinney, Mel. Address to the Suburban Newspapers of America (SNA) Cable TV Seminar, October 1981, at Airlie, VA.

Toffler, Alvin. *The Third Wave.* New York: Bantam Books, Inc., 1981.

Tregoe, Benjamin B., and John W. Zimmerman. *Top Management Strategy.* New York: Simon & Schuster, 1980.

Trienens, Howard J. "Restriction on Publishing Urged by ANPA," *Editor & Publisher* (March 20, 1982).

Udell, Jon. "Newsprint Cost Climbed Faster than Indices," *presstime* (September 1982).

——— *The Economics of the American Newspaper.* New York: Hastings House, 1978.

Urban, Christine D. "Social Impact of Emerging Technologies." Address to the American Press Institute's "Newspapers, Telecommunications and Cable TV" Seminar, September 1982, at Reston, VA.

Urben, Linda. "Cellular Radio to Increase Mobile Phones' Reach," *Publishers' Auxiliary* (April 5, 1982).

Weiss, Barbara J. "Writing for Videotex," *Videotex Canada* (Fall 1983).

Welch, Jim. "Electronic Information Services Blossom Under Dialcom," *Production News* (June 1982).

Whalen, Bernie. "DBS Firms to 'Dish Out' Video Programs to Millions of Homes," *Marketing News* 17 (November 25, 1983).

Wicker, Tom. *On Press.* New York: Viking Press, 1978.

Wright, Donald F. "Electronic Publishing: How to Use it and Why," *presstime* (February 1982).

Wriston, Walter B. "Publishers Go Electronic," *Business Week* (June 11, 1984).

Index

About the Author

David A. Patten is a reporter for KJAC-TV Channel 4 (NBC) in Beaumont-Port Arthur, TX. Formerly, he was the executive director of *Loudoun Times-Mirror* Cable News Channel 33 in Leesburg, VA and the director of long-range planning for Arundel Communications, a suburban Washington, DC weekly newspaper group.

A graduate of the Northwestern University Medill School of Journalism and of the Columbia University Graduate School of Journalism, Mr. Patten first became interested in the relationship of electronic media to print media as a staff writer for *The Ledger Star* in Norfolk, VA.

Related Titles from Knowledge Industry Publications, Inc.

The Future of Videotext: Worldwide Prospects for Home/Office Electronic Information Services
by Efrem Sigel, *et al.*
ISBN 0-86729-025-0   hardcover $34.95

The Birth of Electronic Publishing: Legal and Economic Issues in Telephone, Cable and Over-the-Air Teletext and Videotext
by Richard M. Neustadt
ISBN 0-86729-030-7   hardcover $32.95

After Divestiture: What the AT&T Settlement Means for Business and Residential Telephone Service
by Samuel A. Simon
ISBN 0-86729-110-9   hardcover $34.95

Protecting Privacy in Two-Way Electronic Services
by David H. Flaherty
ISBN 0-86729-107-9   hardcover $34.95

Electronic Publishing Plus
by Martin Greenberger
ISBN 0-86729-146-X   hardcover $45.00

Electronic Marketing: Emerging TV and Computer Channels for Interactive Home Shopping
by Lawrence Strauss
ISBN 0-86729-023-4   hardcover $34.95

Who Owns the Media?
by Benjamin M. Compaine
ISBN 0-86729-007-2   hardcover $45.00

Guide to Electronic Publishing
by Fran Spigai and Peter Sommer
ISBN 0-914236-87-3   softcover $95.00

Available from Knowledge Industry Publications, Inc., 701 Westchester Ave., White Plains, NY 10604.